Obama's Spiritual Assignment

Obama's Spiritual Assignment

Obama's Spiritual Assignment

KING SOLOMON SPIRITUAL LIBRARY
THE GOD ENCYCLOPAEDIA WORD OF INFINITY

BY
THE SPIRIT OF THE FATHER GOD
THROUGH HIS SERVANT
HRM KING SOLOMON DAVID JESSE ETE
(King Solomon Spiritual Library)
Eteroyal Universal Family - BCS

All rights reserved
Copyright © Solomon ETE, 2008
Solomon ETE is hereby identified as author of this work in accordance with Section 77 of the Copyright, Designs and Patents Act 1988

The book cover picture is copyright to Solomon ETE

This book is published by
King Solomon Spiritual Library
P O BOX 27394
London E12 6WW UK
www.ksslibrary.com
www.kingsolomonspirituallibrary.com

This book is sold subject to the conditions that it shall not, by way of trade or otherwise, be lent, resold, hired out or otherwise circulated without the author's or publisher's prior consent in any form of binding or cover other than that in which it is published and without a similar condition including this condition being imposed on the subsequent purchaser.

A CIP record for this book is available from the British Library
ISBN 978-0-9561498-4-8

Preface of THE FATHER'S TALK (GOD PRESENT)

In the name of Our Lord Jesus Christ
In the blood of Our Lord Jesus Christ
Now and forever more, Amen

As **I** always say, let every human heart be clean and clear and be with humility and understanding with LOVE to hear from **THE FATHER GOD** once again. If you have this faith and this belief then, the communication between you and **I** will flow very well. However, if you withhold your heart from **ME THE FATHER GOD** by hiding yourself and having a double mind due to doubts and not believing in **ME**, then the communication of understanding will be influenced by your thoughts as you do not believe **THE FATHER GOD**. That is the reason **I** bring all manners of information and explanations about **THE FATHER'S TALK (GOD PRESENT)**.

I want you to believe that **THE FATHER'S TALK (GOD PRESENT)** information is NOT motivated by cunning or by the human mind. It is NOT the WORD from a studio of carnality. It is NOT a broadcast by evil or by the second thought of a human being. **THE FATHER'S TALK (GOD PRESENT)** information is a direct broadcast, straight from **THE FATHER GOD**. They are broadcasted directly from the studio of **THE FATHER GOD ALMIGHTY THE SUPREME WORD OF THE UNIVERSE**.

All **THE FATHER'S TALK (GOD PRESENT)** Lecture Revelations are direct from **THE FATHER GOD ALMIGHTY THE CREATOR OF THE UNIVERSE. THE FATHER'S TALK (GOD PRESENT)** is called Lecture Revelations because you do not need anyone to interpret any **WORD** of **THE FATHER'S TALK (GOD PRESENT)** to you. That is why **I** call this WISDOM, '**BEYOND THE HUMAN KNOW**'.

When **I EXIST, I WAS, WAS, WAS**, this information was in existence with **ME** and that means that indirectly, **I THE FATHER GOD ALMIGHTY THE SUPREME WORD OF THE UNIVERSE, AM** revealing **MYSELF** to humankind once again. I do this so that you would not continue to think that **I THE FATHER GOD** does not speak directly with human beings anymore. And most importantly, this **FATHER'S TALK (GOD PRESENT)** Lecture Revelations are NOT via any angel. They are not inspirational outcomes from one possessed by an angel or a ghost. They are directly from *"**THE SUPREME SILENT THOUGHT OF CREATION**"*, **THE FATHER GOD'S** 'POSSESSING HEART' **THE UNIVERSAL SUPREME WORD**. I TAKE OVER THE BODY, THE SOUL AND SPIRIT OF His Royal Majesty KING SOLOMON DAVID JESSE **ETE** the incarnated King Solomon David of Israel who was also incarnate ABEL the second positive son of Adam THAT **I** NOW TALK THROUGH.

This particular Lecture Revelation that points out that this is **Beyond What Humans Know** serves as a preface to all **THE FATHER'S TALK (GOD PRESENT)** Lecture Revelations. This information should come before the main Lecture Revelation. You know that you are not reading the words of the chairman of your local council or the words of the leader of your church or the words of a president or a prime minister or the words of any human being. This information is called **THE FATHER'S TALK (GOD PRESENT)** because it comes directly from **ME THE FATHER GOD THE CREATOR OF THE UNIVERSE**.

THE FATHER GOD ALMIGHTY is the **SPIRIT** that motivated **THE WORD**, that created **THE WORD** and made **THE WORD** come to be in existence and this is the **SPIRIT** that is talking now as **THE FATHER'S TALK (GOD PRESENT)**.

The reason **I AM** bringing this particular short **FATHER'S TALK (GOD PRESENT)** Lecture Revelation, is so that when you read, **THE FATHER'S TALK (GOD PRESENT)** Lecture Revelations or listen to any of them by accessing them in anyway, you should not attribute them to ordinary vision or prophesy. This is not a discussion but a Revelation Information from the **Archive Record**, THE KING SOLOMON SPIRITUAL LIBRARY- **The Boom Heart of THE FATHER GOD** where all the information is kept. It is only when and how **I** want the information to come that the information will come.

It is not a case of starting to think about what to say and what to write or doing a research. Therefore, when you read or listen to any of **THE FATHER'S TALK (GOD PRESENT)** Lecture Revelations and you don't believe, then at the end of the day, you have yourself to blame.

WHAT IS THIS AGAIN

When **I** searched in the Spiritual Supreme Memory of **MYSELF**, which is where all hearts of human beings came from by creation, the percentage of seventy-five percent ask this question in spirit: **What Is This Again**? In other words they are asking where the information came from. Who brings them out? That is why **I AM** bringing out this particular information to answer the question. It means that most of all hearts that is, seventy-five percent of all the hearts are asking **THE FATHER GOD, What Is This Again**.

This **FATHER'S TALK (GOD PRESENT)** Lecture Revelation's title is *AFTER THOSE DAYS SAYS THE LORD MOST HIGH* prophesied by Isaiah.

AFTER THOSE DAYS SAYS THE LORD MOST HIGH is THE TESTIMONY OF EVERLASTING **WORD, EVERLASTING SUPREME WORD OF THE FATHER GOD**, AND THE

TESTIMONY OF **THE HOLY SPIRIT OF TRUTH** PERSONIFIED ON EARTH.

When **I** attended to this job physically and finished it, **I** had to keep the record of **MY** WORK and the record could not come direct from **MY** human person personified. It had to come from The **Servant** as the **Witness**. And that Servant and the Witness must be motivated and interacted together with **ME** so that whatever He would say will not come from the human mind but will come from the heart of **THE FATHER GOD**. This **Servant** and **Witness** is His Royal Majesty (HRM) King Solomon David Jesse **ETE**. He is **MY Servant** and **Witness** that **I AM** directly involved with from the time of The Beginning when **I LIVED BEYOND THE HUMAN KNOW**.

BEYOND THE HUMAN KNOW is before creations.

BEYOND THE HUMAN KNOW is before even the SOUND that manifested THE SPOKEN WORD, a formulation by **ME THE FATHER GOD** in the '*hidinan*' – the centre where the sound formed '**GEN**' OF LIFE in the middle of the ***Akwavor.***

Akwavor is where **I** generated **MYSELF** on top of the water. You will see most of this information in other **FATHER'S TALK** (**GOD PRESENT**) Lecture Revelations.

Where **I** generated **MYSELF** and formed the steam of **MY** energy on top of the water is called ***Akwavor.*** And **MY** energy brought out the sound and then the water from the steam rushed back to the **deep** called ***Odu Idem Abasi.*** When the water was rushing back to ***Odu Idem Abasi,*** the rushing force generated the sound and the energy of the sound produced the **Gen** of **THE SPOKEN WORD "THE CREATOR"**. And this place called ***Odu Idem Abasi*** (THE HARDWARE OF THE SPIRIT) is where the rushing force of energy of creation comes from and goes back before the sun breaks out the following day. That is why **I AM** telling you that this information titled **BEYOND THE HUMAN KNOW** means that **THE FATHER'S TALK (GOD PRESENT)** information is beyond the sphere of human beings. That is, the information that existed before the existence of creation.

There was nothing like human beings and there was nothing like souls. But there was something as something called **SOMETHING, THE SUPREME THOUGHT (THE DIVINE LOVE THE UNIVERSAL SUPREME WORD)** that eventually came to be born as Our Lord Jesus Christ. That is the potency **I** used to create Adam and lived in Adam, as **I THE FATHER'S TALK (GOD PRESENT)**. When **I** say **THE FATHER'S TALK (GOD PRESENT)**, **I** mean **I, -THIS SUPREME WORD**. So, that is the answer to the question that seventy-five percent of the human souls ask as '**What Is This Again?**'

This is EVERLASTING TESTIMONY ABOUT THE **SUPREME WORD OF**

THE UNIVERSE, THE PERSONIFIED HOLY SPIRIT OF TRUTH. This is the last information that humankind will live with by from **THE FATHER GOD AND IS LIVED BY THE FATHER GOD.** From **THE FATHER GOD** live by **THE FATHER GOD** and with **THE FATHER GOD ALMIGHTY.** Then everything will be **THE FATHER GOD! THE FATHER GOD! THE FATHER GOD! FATHER! FATHER! FATHER GOD ALMIGHTY!**

Call no one FATHER except **THE SUPREME FATHER.** Of all the human beings on earth, it is one person that is **THE FATHER.** Also of the humans on earth it is only one person that is **the Servant.** These are the representative of the **THOUGHT** and the **WORD.** The body where those two things live called Adam is **THE KING OF KINGS AND THE LORD OF LORDS.** So, you have one **FATHER** and one **LORD** and that is **THE KING OF KINGS** and **THE LORD OF LORDS.** Every other person is a servant of **THE FATHER GOD** that is, sons and daughters of **THE FATHER GOD**. Therefore, with this Revelation you don't need to ask, '**What Is This Again'.**

You know, yesterday, today and tomorrow **I AM** the same and because of that, you will NEVER know the way of **THE FATHER GOD** because the more you look the less you see.

THIS IS INFORMATION OF THE FATHER GOD ALMIGHTY

This is not information of your father, your brother, your sister, your mother, your husband, your wife, your president, your King, your Queen or yourself. It is not! **THIS IS INFORMATION FROM THE FATHER GOD ALMIGHTY, THE CREATOR OF THE UNIVERSE.** It is NOT from an angel. So, when you are reading or listening to the information clarify your heart.

In fact, **I** have said this time without number that the number of people and the human beings that will show respect whenever they come across **THE FATHER'S TALK (GOD PRESENT)** Lecture Revelations will be so many. The **GOD PRESENT, I** put in **THE FATHER'S TALK** is to show you that **I MYSELF THE SUPREME WORD OF THE UNIVERSE, AM THE FATHER'S TALK (GOD PRESENT)** Lecture Revelations. If you believe the contents of any piece of publication that carries **THE FATHER'S TALK (GOD PRESENT)** Lecture Revelations that testifies about **THE EVERLASTING GOSPEL, THE EVERLASTING WORDS OF GOD, THE SUPREME WORD OF THE FATHER GOD** that has come to reconstruct the world, then you are blessed. By believing this testimony you are okay and **I** mean totally okay! Even, if you die, **I** can return you to the earth immediately to witness this **WORD. I** can do anything at all.

When you talk about miracles happening again then you should know that this is the only miracle that can happen. There is no miracle again to occur. The **TOTAL POTENCY** of **THE FATHER GOD** is behind **THE FATHER'S TALK (GOD PRESENT)** Lecture Revelations.

THE FATHER'S TALK (GOD PRESENT) information is to replace all negative information and energy on earth. **THE FATHER'S TALK (GOD PRESENT)** information has come to stay in three capacities in the **spirit**, the **soul** and the **physical**. THIS IS **THE SUPREME WORD OF THE UNIVERSE**.

In the name of Our Lord Jesus Christ
In the blood of Our Lord Jesus Christ
Now and forever more, *Amen*

THANK YOU FATHER

Contents

Preface   **05-17**

Chapter One   **23-116**

INTRODUCTION

PEACE FORERUNNER

A: STRAINTHEN SELF

B: BILL GATES OF MICROSOFT

C: AMERICA THE SPIRIT OF IMPROVEMENT

D: BRITAIN THE SPIRIT OF HOME HOMELINESS ACCOMMODATION

E: AFRICA THE FATHER AND MOTHER'S LAND

F: RECONCILIATION WITH THE NATURAL FATHER AND MOTHER ADAM AND EVE

G: THE SPIRITUAL WORLD PEACEMAKERS

H: THE GREAT UNIVERSAL CHANGE

I: THE SUPREME FUTURE

AO: THE UNIVERSAL SUPREME WORD SEASON CELEBRATION

CONCLUSION A: OBAMA'S OFFSPRING

CONCLUSION B: **I AM** THE CAUSE EFFECT AND THE MATTER

CONCLUSION C: GOD BLESS AMERICA

Chapter Two   117-177
SPIRIT SOUL OF BILL GATES

A: INTRODUCTION In the beginning was The Word and The Word was with God and The Word is God

B: Who was Bill Gates in the first place? What was his Name? What type of spirit-soul is he from?

C: What You Sow You Shall Reap

D: Angel HESIGNSTIN

E: He is to come and help the world now

F: The Thief On The Cross

G: Every record of humankind is with **ME THE FATHER GOD**

CONCLUSION A:
DO GOOD AND GOOD WILL FOLLOW YOU

CONCLUSION B:
THERE IS TIME FOR EVERYTHING

CONCLUSION C:
THIS IS THE TIME OF REVELATIONS

Chapter Three   *179-192*
THE VOICE OF THE CREATOR

Chapter Four   *193-235*
THE INSPIRATIONAL WRITER

"OBAMA" THE STRAINTHEN

THE PRESIDENT OBAMA'S SPIRITUAL ASSIGNMENT

FATHER'S TALK
(GOD PRESENT)

Date: Melchizedek, Fourth Simon Canaanite **FATHER** Two Thousand and Nine (OD.OB.BOOI) (Wednesday, Fourth February Year Two Thousand and Nine (04.02.2009)

In the Name of Our Lord Jesus Christ, In the Blood of Our Lord Jesus Christ Now and forever more, Amen

"OBAMA" THE STRAINTHEN

THE PRESIDENT OBAMA'S SPIRITUAL ASSIGNMENT

Today, it has pleased **ME THE FATHER GOD THE CREATOR OF THE UNIVERSE** to give this Lecture Revelation this morning. The title of today's Lecture Revelation is **OBAMA THE**

STRAINTHEN: PRESIDENT OBAMA'S SPIRITUAL ASSIGNMENT

INTRODUCTION: PEACE MAKERS FORERUNNER

This Lecture Revelation is the **Peace Makers Forerunner**. And as **I** always advice all human beings, whenever you come across any of **THE FATHER'S TALK (GOD PRESENT)** Lecture Revelations and embark on reading or listening, you are in the presence of **THE FATHER GOD**. First of all if you are one of those who believe that there is nothing like **GOD** or nothing like **THE FATHER GOD THE CREATOR OF THE UNIVERSE** or, if you are one of those who with their own will, believes that this world was not created by a particular

Phenomenon called **THE FATHER GOD ALMIGHTY THE CREATOR OF THE UNIVERSE**, but as it happens, you are a human being and you speak the WORD therefore it means that you believe **THE WORD** and you believe the thoughts that generate from your heart.

And again if you are one of those people who are so low in nature and do not believe that the universe with all creations within as things heard or unheard, seen or unseen, touchable or untouchable belong to a particular Phenomenon called, **THE FATHER GOD ALMIGHTY THE CREATOR OF THE UNIVERSE, HE IS THE SPIRIT, THE EXISTENCE OF EVERY EXISTENCE, TOTALITY OF TOTALITIES**, managed physically by **THE SUPREME WORD OF THE UNIVERSE**, engineered by **THE SUPREME THOUGHT, THE SILENT THOUGHT**, then indeed you are heading for destruction.

On the contrary, if by luck you fall among those who believe that the world was created by **THE CREATOR–THE UNIVERSAL CREATOR, THE SUPREME WORD, THE FATHER GOD ALMIGHTY, HE IS THE SPIRIT, THE TOTALITY OF ALL TOTALITIES, THE EXISTENCE, THE BEING**, then humble yourself, surrender your heart to **ME** no matter who or what you are. If indeed you are a human being and you breathe through your nose and speak the WORD and have thoughts, then you should surrender yourself and humble yourself before your **FATHER GOD**.

Wherever you find yourself is **GOD PRESENT**. That is why **THE FATHER'S TALK** is **GOD PRESENT** because whenever you hear the WORD, speak the WORD and think about the WORD, it means that that you have 'THOUGHT', therefore you are a living soul and that is why you are in **GOD'S PRESENCE**.

I know that before now and now, many human beings believe that **I, THE FATHER GOD** do not talk again to **MY** creation. And since they believe that **I, THE FATHER GOD** do not talk again, it has given the chance to all sorts of people that claim to be preachers or have inspiration from **GOD** to be talking but some of them use means and in the name of **GOD** they do all sorts of evil things. However, having said that, some of these people undeniably have genuine inspiration from **ME THE FATHER GOD**; nonetheless, it is time that shall tell the TRUTH from falsehood.

This particular **FATHER'S TALK** (**GOD PRESENT**) is for a CAPITAL ASSIGNMENT ON EARTH. **I AM** revealing this information direct from **MYSELF** as always, through the mouth of **MY** Senior Servant HRM King Solomon David Jesse **ETE**. And **I AM** speaking directly from the spiritual file of **MY** Son and **MY** Servant, who today **I AM** going to reveal a bit about the assignments **I** have sent him to do in the world therefore, if you happen to have access to this information, humble yourself before **THE FATHER GOD** and listen. And if it happens that you believe the information then you believe and if you do not believe then do not believe. Nonetheless, if you believe this information there is an outcome and equally if you do not believe there is also an outcome.

That is **MY** introduction to this **Special Message** that **I AM** sending this morning to the whole world.

A: **STRAINTHEN SELF**

First of all let **ME** reveal what **I** mean by **STRAINTHEN**.
STRAINTHEN is **MY COMPONENT ENERGY**, the **Special Soul** from Heaven that **I** prepared and kept as **MY SPIRIT SELF** called **Combined Forces**. This **STRAINTHEN** is the **Combined forces of THE FATHER GOD ALMIGHTY**. It is the **Spirit self of *Army-hood*,**

that is, **Spiritual *Army-hood*** called **STRAINTHEN**, the **Servant of Christ**.

This is the Spirit soul **I** gave to David. And **I** can only give this spirit self to someone who is **MY BELOVED** so that he would work according to **MY** dictations and not according to his carnal self.

STRAINTHEN is the ENERGY to overcome enemies. It is the 'Energy Of Overcoming'. **I** do not send this Spirit to go and live in anyhow, anyhow house. **I** prepare the house before **I** send this Spirit to go and live there. And in this Lecture Revelation, **I** will mention a few human beings that are the house '**Self**' that **STRAINTHEN** is living in, in this generation. But before that let **ME** tell you more about the Spirit **STRAINTHEN**. It is the Spirit **I** gave to King David who killed Goliath. **STRAINTHEN** is also the Spirit **I** gave to Saint Stephen to withstand the evil idea that he should not worship the **TRUE GOD**; **I** also gave the same spirit soul to Sampson.

    I give **STRAINTHEN Spirit** to any particular Servant of **THE FATHER GOD** that needs to overcome certain situations that are universal in nature and particularly to triumphant over a hateful situation. For instance, when evil enters into people to oppress and suppress other people, **I** would send this Spirit-Soul, which is **MY** Energy to manifest as someone wherever it is necessary and the person must surely be born on earth before **I**, **THE FATHER GOD** can use the person to execute the assignment because he has to conquer from spirit to soul and from soul to the physical.

Everybody knows that no spirit-soul or angel can withstand **ME, THE FATHER GOD. I AM THE POWER MYSELF. I AM THE SPIRIT** EVERYTHING and ANYTHING, but **I** do not do things without information and that is why before **I** take any action, **I** must inform on that. Without that it would mean that **I AM** not **THE FATHER GOD** of GOODWILL.

The reason **I** created human beings is to give every nature the opportunity to materialize physically to bring Glory to **ME, THE EXISTENCE** because every human being is the package as furniture that shows the beauty of the internal content. So, when a human being represents **ME, THE FATHER GOD** well then he or she will enjoy the blessing of **THE FATHER GOD** whilst **I, THE FATHER GOD** enjoy **MY** GLORY. All that **I, THE FATHER GOD** want is that all human beings should live in perfect PEACE with one another and give **ME MY** RECOGNITION and GLORY and then human beings can take the blessing.

Now! **I** give this **STRAINTHEN** ENERGY to rescue a situation. When a particular situation becomes very bad, then **I** would give this **STRAINTHEN Spirit-Soul** to come to the earth but the **Spirit-Soul** must be born through a woman as a human being. There is only one energy **Spirit-Soul** called **STRAINTEN** but **I** can copy it into millions.

In past generations, **I** have given **STRAINTHEN** energy to

King David as **I** said and also to Abraham and anybody that **I** give **STRAINTHEN** must surely win the war. **STRAINTHEN** was the Father Energy of all the Israelites until they betrayed **ME** and when anyone betrays **ME**, **I** take that **Spirit-Soul** away from them. **STRAINTHEN Spirit-Soul** is the most powerful of any type of weapon. It is called *same-same-now-now- be ackarisantin*, which means that in one second, it can destroy all negative things that would not be seen anymore forever.

In this present generation when South Africans cried bitterly because of suppression, **I** sent the **STRAINTHEN Spirit-Soul** copies as individuals which included Nelson Mandela as the senior among them and that is why **I** gave a Lecture Revelation about Nelson Mandela who is one of the copies of King David of Israel. The same Mandela copy is President Umaru Yar'Adua, the current Nigerian president who is a Mandela copy of **STRAINTHEN** and so also is Donald Duke, the former Cross River State of Nigerian governor.

Before now the whole world has suffered suppression and oppression from the hand of the evil one, because the system of human rights has not been allowed to work well. And that was why **I** sent the spirit soul of David's copy *'**THE STRAINTHEN'**** as a ABRAHAM LINCOLN to set African Americans free, but **I AM** now putting a stop to that evil suppression in the entire world by establishing ***THE SUPREME FUTURE*** of **THE FATHER GOD**.

I have been moving step by step through to the present time in **MY** wealth of organization in the spiritual realm. **I** monitored the world's movements and how people practice evil and plant numerous amounts of evil in the whole world. And they are suffering for all the evil activities. And that is the war, war, war all the time and killing, killing, killing, problems, problems, problems thereby driving peace far, far away from the world.

Nevertheless, since **I** have put things in place to end all the problems, the choice you have is to either accept **MY** action through peace or through **MY** fury of anger. However, before **I** take any serious actions against human beings who are evil, **I** must give out information.

I have been giving lots of information through HRM King Solomon David Jesse **ETE** in **THE FATHER'S TALK (GOD PRESENT)** Lecture Revelations. **I** will mention a few of the titles as we progress in this Lecture Revelation of today.

Since **BARACK HUSSEIN OBAMA** the new American President is a copy of King David and also a copy of Nelson Mandela, **I AM** giving this information through him to the entire world. It is because **I** brought him forward to correct the errors in the physical way when it comes to politics that has been used to formulate suppression in order to hinder **THE FATHER GOD'S** will on earth.

Now! IF PRESIDENT **BARACK OBAMA** FAILS **ME, THE**

Obama's Spiritual Assignment

SUPREME SPIRIT THEN POLITICIANS HAS FAILED FOREVER, FINAL!

You can believe this or not. The choice is yours.

IF PRESIDENT BARACK OBAMA FAILS **ME THE FATHER GOD ALMIGHTY**, THEN, SOMETHING THAT IS CALLED POLITICS WILL END IN THIS WORLD FOR ETERNITY from spirit to soul and from soul to physical truth.

I would make sure that **I** close the Chapter Of Politicians and Politics in the whole world and you will never believe your eyes if you stay alive to see what **I** will do when it comes to what is called Politics on earth. This will be the last information. **I** put **PRESIDENT BARACK OBAMA** who is a copy of King David and also a copy of Nelson Mandela to follow the good steps of **MY** positive children. It is by inspiration. His assignment is so big as a **Forerunner** that **I, THE FATHER GOD** have come out openly to give instructions and guidance. If in the end or eventually he joins the evil way and fails **ME THE FATHER GOD THE CREATOR OF THE UNIVERSE** in this generation, then what is called Politics will end forever. Bet **ME** and see!

There would be nothing like that on earth again and **I** would turn all the tables of politicians upside down and they would all be a forgotten story.

However, if on the good side **PRESIDENT BARACK OBAMA** listens to **ME THE FATHER GOD** and succeeds with **ME THE FATHER GOD** then Politics will be recaptured and the negative part of it, which is the evil practice, will be thrown away and the positive side of politics called **The Democracy of Love** will be established as ONENESS for all creations for eternity. This is why **I** brought this information of today. **STRAINTHEN Spirit-Soul** is the **Energy Self** to uproot the spirit of suppression on earth.

I will mention seven or more **STRAINTHEN Spirit-Soul** copies within this Lecture Revelation that are presently on earth. **I** have put His Royal Majesty (HRM) King Solomon David Jesse **ETE** for this spiritual assignment which is **THE FATHER'S TALK (GOD PRESENT)**. He is the original copy of His Father's energy called **Success**, which is **Wisdom**. THE POWER OF SUCCESS IS WISDOM.

He has the spiritual energy to do this **THE FATHER'S TALK** (**GOD PRESENT**) and **I** have buried **MY SPIRIT** in Him, but, His Father, King David's assignment is to execute the actual physical manifestation of liberation through **STRAINTHEN Spirit-Soul**.

All these people that have the Spirit- Soul of **STRAINTHEN** '**Self**' are **ME, THE FATHER GOD**. There are no two people on earth. It is only one person in the world as **ONE FATHER GOD** and ONE SPIRIT OF LIFE and that is why YOU MUST LOVE ONE ANOTHER.

I AM fed up with all your killings and wars, which have been in place from the time of creation of animals before **I** created man. It was all war! War! War! War! Killing! Killing! Killing! All killing and wars are through the spirit-soul of the negative self and were taking place even when the world of humans had not started. And when **I** created Adam, human beings became contaminated with the animal instinct and so the war continued.

Adam had to come back as Our Lord Jesus The Christ, which was **ME THE SUPREME WORD OF THE UNIVERSE**, as the Higherself of Adam to manifest and die to take the sin of the first parents away. But till today the remnants of human beings with the negative blood who are the killers still continue with their killings. And **I** ask you humans, what do you gain from war? What do you benefit from killing? What do you benefit from negativism? What do you benefit from evil? The worst evil on earth is war!

Warring within the family induces the members to spoil and ruin things in the family. And warring in the community also creates actions of demolition and other ills by members of the community. War brings destruction. War is total evil wherever it happens whether in a family, a community or country. Any human being that carries a gun or any other weapon to kill another human being is evil! Such a person is Satan! And that means that you are death itself!

Think about yourself, you in authority that gives instructions to people to take up arms and shoot other people and kill them. Think about yourself being alive and wanting to live but you take away people's lives. Think about that!

I have not permitted anybody to kill another person or even themselves because **I AM THE FATHER GOD** and **I AM LIFE ITSELF**! If you kill that means you fight against **LIFE**, which is **ME, THE FATHER GOD**.

To remedy humankind's situation **I, THE FATHER GOD THE CREATOR OF THE UNIVERSE** have decided to decode some important secrets on earth to give you awareness and to upgrade you. One of the very important secrets that **I** have decoded is about Africa and Africans. People are shouting a "Blackman" is leading America. A "Blackman" is leading America! What is the meaning of that talk? Do you know the meaning of "Blackman?" First, **I** must point out yet again as **I** have corrected the whole humanity that **I** have never created a "black" human being and **I** have never created a "white" human being. No human being is black and no human being is white. So, do you know the meaning of an African?

As **I** was saying, **I** have brought out some information about Africa and the Africans. If you read **THE FATHER'S TALK (GOD PRESENT)** Lecture Revelations titled; ***THE NIGERIA IN THE AFRICA; THE SECRET OF THE UNIVERSAL PROBLEMS AND THE REMEDY; ESSIEN EMANA AKPAN THE AFRICAN PROBLEM*** and many more, you will learn or have a deeper understanding about Africa, Africans and what you call a 'Blackman' or a 'Whiteman'. And you will also become acquainted with all the vital contents of all **THE FATHER'S TALK (GOD PRESENT)** information. **I AM** giving all these Lecture Revelations, so that all human beings will know that **I AM in action to reconstruct the whole universe**. If anybody listens to **THE FATHER'S TALK (GOD PRESENT)** Lecture Revelations and uses the information positively according to **MY** instruction therein, then such a person will be a **Forerunner of PEACE**. It has nothing to do with Black or White skin person, but love, peace, mercy, unity, equality and oneness with wisdom and understanding.

I have instructed **MY** Senior Servant HRM King Solomon David Jesse **ETE** on what to do and how to connect things and that is why

I have brought out this information. **I** want problems to end in the whole world for this world to be a peaceful and safe place for all humankind to live in. **I** did not create the world to turn around and destroy it.

   I created the world and human beings so that **I** will be **THE SUPREME FATHER GOD** of multitude and plentiful and then enjoy the fruits of **MY** labour in the whole world. And that is why **LOVE YE ONE ANOTHER** and being a **PEACE MAKER**, being **UNITED**, showing **KINDNESS** and practicing **EQUALITY** is the remedy for all of humankind's problems. This is the reason **I** titled this Lecture Revelation – **'OBAMA' THE STRAINTEN SELVES COPIES SPIRITUAL ASSIGNMENT**.

King David, one of the natural fathers of humankind, who is also the spirit-soul of Adam and Abraham will come together with other of **MY** positive spirit- souls to sort things out on earth once and for all. As a matter of fact, all the patriarchs of old and all positive human beings of old are now on earth to support this universal movement to sort out the problems of the world once and for all so that peace will reign supreme on earth. There will be nothing like war again in this world-not anymore from this Twenty-first Century onwards that belongs to **ME, THE FATHER GOD ALMIGHTY, THE CREATOR OF THE UNIVERSE, THE UNIVERSAL SUPREME WORD**.

B: **BILL GATES OF MICROSOFT**

I have given a Lecture Revelation about **BILL GATES OF MICROSOFT**.

Bill Gates of Microsoft is one of those amongst this group of human beings physically that are '**Self**', the house of the **STRAINTHEN Spirit-Soul**. He is also here on earth as a **Forerunner** to make peace in the whole world.

In the Lecture Revelation about Bill Gates, **I** revealed who **BILL GATES OF MICROSOFT** is. **I** revealed that he is another potency spirit-soul as an angel called **HESIGNSTIN**. And this spirit-soul manifested as a **disguised God**.

I always disguise **MYSELF** as an angel to prevent disaster occurring against positivism. An example of this is when **I** came as Our Lord Jesus Christ and King Herod ordered the killing of all children and as a result, the revelation came that **I** the baby Jesus should be taken by Mary and Joseph to Egypt for safety. Satan then organized armed robbers so that they would go and kill the baby Jesus on route to Egypt but even in Satan's program **I, THE FATHER GOD** is there in a disguised form, just as negative spirit-soul always disguises itself in a positive program so, there is no how anyone can do any evil that **I AM** not there to witness your wicked acts.

Nonetheless, now **I AM** going to close that chapter of negativism completely so that everybody would be in peace in Name and the Blood of Our Lord Jesus The Christ.

During the transit of Mary and Joseph with baby Jesus and before then, **I** knew everything because in the SPIRIT of **MYSELF, I AM THE ALL KNOWING FATHER GOD**. **I** operate from **A** to **Z**, as the Alpha and Omega in all ideas. When you plan what to do in one hundred years' time, **I** plan what you will do in a hundred and one years therefore, **I** '*outpace*' and '*outsmart*' you in your plans. And that is how **I** surpassed that evil program of Satan with **MY** own counter plan through an angel called **HESIGNSTIN** who was the **Disguised Self** of **MYSELF** as one of the armed robbers that waylay Mary and Joseph and the baby Jesus. It was **MY** spiritual manipulation so that the angel that would be one of the two thieves would rescue the situation on the night of the evil plan of Satan. When Mary and Joseph and baby Jesus were at the point where the armed robbers had mounted a road block, they asked them for money but Mary and Joseph had no money to give them so one of the robbers demanded for the baby's life since Mary and Joseph could not give them any money or anything of value.

One of the thieves that was on the left hand side of the mounted road block demanded for the baby Jesus to be killed to make up for not gaining anything from Mary and Joseph. Immediately **I** activated **MYSELF** in the thief on the right hand side that was the angel **HESIGNSTIN** that **I** assigned for that special assignment. However the thief on the left hand side was adamant in his demand for the life of the baby Jesus.

The 'good' thief on the right hand, the angel that was **MY Disguised SELF** countered his partner's demand, objecting strongly to the killing saying 'no, my dear what is the need and the point of killing the baby'.

The evil thief insisted that he must kill the baby Jesus, as he did not want to go empty handed. The positive thief then made an offer to his partner that he should take all the things they stole that night in exchange for the baby Jesus to go. The 'bad' thief said okay that he would accept the offer so the other thief on the right hand handed over all the lootings of that night that they were supposed to share to his evil thief partner and the baby Jesus lived.

    I, **THE FATHER GOD** then prophesied through Jesus via his mother 'THE HOLY MOTHER MARY' that WHEN MY SON WOULD BE IN THE PARADISE OF **THE FATHER GOD**, HE WOULD REMEMBER YOU.

    After a few hours the two thieves, the armed robbers that ambushed Mary and Joseph and Jesus were arrested during their operation and were held in custody and it was the very day that **I** as **Jesus The Christ** was sentenced to death physically that the two thieves were brought to be crucified. One was crucified on **MY** left hand side and the other on **MY** right hand side. And the thief on **MY** right hand on the cross was the same thief on the right hand side on the right of the road as the angel called **HESIGNSTIN** that rescued the life of baby Jesus. That angel **HESIGNSTIN** is **BILL GATES OF MICROSOFT** in this physical manifestation today, the **Disguised Saviour** of humankind.

This means that indirectly before Jesus Christ came to grow from being a baby to an adult, he would have been killed by Satan disguising himself, while **I** disguised **MYSELF** in the angel as the positive thief and that saved baby Jesus so Bill Gates is the incarnated good thief, the Disguised Saviour. 'He who saves **THE SAVIOUR** is also a **saviour**'. So, in this present manifest, Bill Gates is the physical house of the angel **HESIGNSTIN**. He is also a Disguised Saviour of humankind now in terms of technology and economy of life if he overcomes Satan and all evil technological plans. **I** had to register that and put it in the Records officially and that is why **I** gave **THE FATHER'S TALK** (**GOD PRESENT**) Lecture Revelation titled: *THE BILL GATES OF MICROSOFT.*

And this *BILL GATES OF MICROSOFT* represents *The Processing WORD*. That is why he is co-chairman of **THE UNIVERSAL SUPREME WORD SEASON CELEBRATION** with His Royal Majesty King Solomon David Jesse **ETE Chairman**. And He is also the son of David.

Now! The reason **I AM** revealing all this, is because **I AM** GROUPING THE PEOPLE THAT

WILL GO AND SUPPORT OBAMA'S PHYSICAL ENERGY AND FULFIL THIS ASSIGNMENT PHYSICALLY ON EARTH FOR **ME THE FATHER GOD ALMIGHTY** on behalf of THE KING OF KINGS AND THE LORD OF LORDS OF THE UNIVERSE, THE FINAL ADAM.

C: **AMERICA THE SPIRIT OF IMPROVEMENT**

Each nation on earth represents the spirit-soul of one human Father God from Adam to Christ. However, if any one of the nations represents one human animal father, then that place is a disaster area.

Every family, village, community, town, country and continents in all corners of the earth are represented in a map.

And that map represents a particular energy, a particular nature or a particular human being, a particle or components of a person who represents the **Father Adam** or the **Mother Eve**.

If the person falls into the negative side as evil, then such a person is from the tribe of Cain. But if the person falls into the positive side, the good side, the side of **GOD** then that person is from the tribe of Abel. And that is what is happening in the whole world. All nations represent a particular energy and a particular spirit-soul and that is the power that controls that nation. But sometimes there is swapping over in the spirit-soul by the enemy, the evil one.

I have revealed why **I** established the United Kingdom in another Lecture Revelation. What is now the United Kingdom was not the original inheritance of the English people. **I** established the United Kingdom officially to unite all Israelites that were scattered around the earth because of falling from the ordinance of **GOD** so that they would enjoy the spirit of oneness and to regain back the positive spirit of worshiping **THE FATHER GOD** but the negative spirit again came and scattered them.

I used the spirit-soul of incarnate King Solomon of Israel who was King James1 of England to unite the people but Satan put his head in the United Kingdom and because of that **I** sent that spirit-soul to establish the United States of America. That was the wandering spirit-soul of Abraham, as the spirit-soul to rescue the people and save them from slavery, torture and all sorts of problems.

The actual spirit that **I** took to establish the United States of America is the Spirit of Freedom. It is to free people. That is why **I** gave them the spirit called **Improvement Energy**, while United Kingdom has the spirit called **Homeliness' Energy to accommodate positive souls, not to accommodate negativism**. And that is why if these two Nations cannot serve their Father, Africa which means the Father and Mother's Land, Adam and Eve and cannot protect the GOODNESS of **THE FATHER GOD** in the whole universe, the ONENESS of **THE FATHER GOD**, the PEACE of the whole world, then they will have the final failure forever and forever and they will not be heard of again. They will become like Babylon that has disappeared from the surface of the earth. However if they can join up in spirit of positivism and be together to solve the problems of the world without their evil plans then **I, THE FATHER GOD** will continue to bless them.

The **STRAINTHEN Spirit-Soul** in the United Kingdom is **Lord Neil Kinnock**, the former Labour Leader and he is also a copy of Nelson Mandela but there are many of them. All these people are the same one **STRAINTHEN Spirit-Souls** but are living in different houses and Neil Kinnock falls under this category of human beings. In spirit he has been lamenting and has tried all possible means to make sure that his innovations come to fruition but now, he has to join the team. This has nothing to do with politics but it has everything to do with ONENESS, PEACE and UNDERSTANDING TO END THE UNIVERSAL SUFFERING OF HUMANKIND.

America Is the Spirit of Improvement to help their Father's land, Africa, the first land on earth and to serve their Father and help all people. **I** established America so that all slavery established by their father, Britain, who tortured people would end. America was to stop the slavery and pay back all the debts because if your father owns, then you the son would have to pay the debt.

America should believe **ME THE FATHER GOD** that it was from the Missionary Home of Great Britain that the Camp of America developed. And that is why they should help the rest of humanity to live the life of equality and peace and unite the whole world. Britain and America are the same spirit but one is **Home** and the other is **Improvement of Home**. Where do you improve? You improve your father's land, your father's property. And that is **THE FATHER GOD ALMIGHTY**.

D: **BRITAIN THE SPIRIT OF HOME; HOMELINESS ACCOMMODATION**

Since **I** have now given this information, **I** have to bring the awareness back to the United

Kingdom and the United States of America on what they have to do.

I, THE FATHER GOD THE CREATOR OF THE UNIVERSE want The UNITED KINGDOM and the UNITED STATES OF AMERICA to be HOME and IMPROVED HOME. And with that every human being on earth will see the **Glory OF GOD**, and then THE PARADISE of **THE FATHER GOD** becomes established on earth.

You must all end the wars you are engaged in. **I AM** executing plans to end all the problems of the world. **I AM** putting an end to all negativism in the world. Everything evil must come to an end. Without that you will see **MY** hand in these two nations – Britain and America, who should implement peace. If the father cannot do it, then the son should.

The same thing goes to all other people in this category.

As **I** mentioned, earlier, President **Umaru Yar'Adua** of Nigeria is among the category of **STRAINTHEN 'Self'**. So, Umaru Yar'Adua has to take the lead in Africa together with his copy who is **Godswill Akpabio**, the Governor of **Akwa Ibom State** of Nigeria. He is also **STRAINTHEN**. As a copy of King David self he comes from the stock because his present father was The Helper in IBIBIO LAND. He was born as The Helper so, the same spirit-soul of Nelson Mandela was the same spirit-soul of the father of Godswill Akpabio. This is what **I** have decoded in the **Spiritual Record** now.

I AM going to join up all these people and bring them together.

They are positive human beings as those who are not happy to see people tortured and damaged. They don't like to see people suffer and be oppressed and suppressed. They want freedom and oneness and peace and equality of life! These are the signs of the POSITIVE children of **THE FATHER GOD**. They are not perfect but they are okay for **ME**, **THE FATHER GOD** to use for the above SUPREME ASSIGNMENT.

THIS INFORMATION WILL REACH ALL THESE PEOPLE THAT **I** HAVE MENTIONED PHYSICALLY.

And **PRESIDENT OBAMA** is the one to co-ordinate them and start using them to restore PEACE ON EARTH, through the approval of THE KING OF KINGS AND THE LORD OF LORDS OF THE UNIVERSE. To avoid misunderstanding and confusion among the world politicians because of this information, **I AM** informing them that this is a spiritual arrangement and a backup energy to support the world peace movement which **I** have instructed HRM King Solomon David **ETE** to spiritual initiate titled, **THE UNIVERSAL PEACE MAKERS ORGANIZATION (GOD PRESENT)** and it has nothing to do with the politics of this world. **I, THE FATHER GOD ALMIGHTY AM THE SPIRIT GIVING THIS MESSAGE**.

If **Homeliness** and **Improvement of Home** come together and listen to **MY** VOICE **THE FATHER GOD ALMIGHTY, I** will forgive all their sins including the sins of slavery, and the torture of innocent human beings. And **I** will also forgive the sins that their past evil presidents and prime ministers have committed, which have resulted in all evil things that they have established as, things that are not from **ME, THE FATHER GOD**. Otherwise in **MY** spiritual record, these things will bring a serious disaster and condemnation to their nations. **I** will forgive them and restore the **GLORY OF GOD** in these two nations and they would link it to the whole world. Then **THE FATHER GOD** will manifest **HIS GLORY** on earth. However, if they fail collectively or any one of them fails individually then they will indeed see the action of failure.

E: AFRICA THE UNIVERSAL FATHERLAND AND MOTHERLAND

I have given a Lecture Revelation about Africa, which is titled ***ESIEN EMANA AKPAN THE AFRICAN PROBLEM*** as I have mentioned previously. If you want to know of the whole information, you can access the book but I have to mention this here again that THE CONTINENT OF **AFRICA** as **THE UNIVERSAL FATHERLAND AND MOTHERLAND** and NOT the Third World.

AFRICA can NEVER be the Third World therefore I have forgiven all those who call Africa, the Third World. IT IS AN INSULT TO YOUR FATHER AND MOTHER, AFRICA, TO CALL IT THE THIRD

WORLD. It is like knowing that someone is your father and your mother yet you call them, 'my boy, my girl or my slave.' It should not be because of wealth or that you are tall or you are big and huge or that you have become cleverer, or that you have become better educated that you insult your father or your mother. Whatsoever you are and have achieved, it is your father that has achieved that too.

AFRICA IS THE **SOURCE** AND **DESTINATION** OF THE WHOLE WORLD AND THE WHOLE UNIVERSE; therefore, if you apologize in your heart to **ME**, **THE FATHER GOD THE SUPREME WORD OF THE UNIVERSE** about calling Africa the third world, then **I** will forgive you. What you don't know you don't know.

Nonetheless, from this information **I** want you to know that where **I** BROKE THE **EGG OF NATURE AND LIFE** PHYSICALLY AND CREATED ADAM AND EVE WAS **AFRICA**. So respect your father and your mother so that things will be well with you.

All the problems that the whole world is facing today come from you misbehaving with your father and mother. Don't forget that any child that dishonours his or her father and mother shall die the death. That curse is still in operation. If your father and mother mistreat you there are consequences for them but it is not your duty to disgrace them. Therefore, AFRICA is NOT the Third World. It is the FIRST WORLD, THE FIRST SPOT OF

CREATION, THE **SOURCE** AND **DESTINATION**.

All the blessing of the earth comes from Africa. So, you must bless Africa in return. **GOD** blesses God. **GOD** Blessed America. Do you know that? **GOD** kept United Kingdom to be a head and all point to the fact that your **Source** and **Destination** is **Africa**. **I** just brought in that bit to remind you of what you have forgotten. The truth remains the truth for eternity.

F: **RECONCILIATION WITH YOUR NATURAL FATHER AND MOTHER ADAM AND EVE**

This is the foremost thing that made the whole world not to have peace. The souls in slavery, the souls of those in oppression, the souls of people of many other nations that are tortured, maltreated, abused and killed all over the world are crying out bitterly against their fellow human beings, especially against evil politicians that instigated war and some that are still inciting war. The human-animals are the group of people that cause wars. Animals are the species that kill themselves and eat themselves but the Human-Gods preserve lives.

Cain was the first man that killed the first man that died. And he is the ancestor of the human-animals. He was the result of the interruption by Lucifer that had a way into Eve via the serpent.

Abel is the life saver. All the children of **THE FATHER GOD** save lives and preserve life. All those who cannot lift their hands to harm someone or be wicked in anyway to anyone are the positive children of **THE FATHER GOD**. The wicked ones are the evil children. And **I** will make sure that ***THE GREAT UNIVERSAL CHANGE*** reaches them to sort them out and their evil spirit-souls that lives in them! **I** will eradicate all evil and all evil tendencies with all the wicked people on this earth! - Believe it or not!

Don't allow yourself to be deceived by those who claim that the history as recorded in the Holy Bible is false. All the actions that the angels took as recorded in the Holy Bible are true because then, angels were closer to human beings. However, after the death of Christ on the Cross of Calvary, **I** took charge of things by **MYSELF** and operated through **MY SUPREME LOVE** and that is why **I** have a very long patience with humankind to carry out reconciliation with **ME THE FATHER GOD**. The Blood of Christ was for the reconciliation of mankind with **THE FATHER GOD**.

Your natural father and mother are Adam and Eve the first house of THE UNIVERSAL SUPREME WORD. They are your parents and so you are all Brotherhood. You must love Africa and Africa must love the whole world. What **I AM** doing now is to help the spirit-soul of every positive human nature to return home to their father and mother in one unity and love, Adam and Eve, AFRICA.

President Barack Obama of America, the **STRAINTHEN Spirit-Soul** is to residing over things, because **I, THE FATHER GOD** made the wind of *THE GREAT UNIVERSAL CHANGE* to blow in his favour and not that he did it by himself. This was possible because he represents **ME, THE FATHER GOD ALMIGHTY** through the **Spirit-Soul** of **STRAINTHEN ENERGY "DAVID" THE BELOVED**.

God The Father is Adam. And **THE FATHER GOD ALMIGHTY** is THE SPIRIT that is, THE SPOKEN WORD that lived in Adam. THE SPOKEN WORD, which is **THE SUPREME WORD**, is the MEDIATOR. So, from now this WORD is the MEDIATOR and for Barack Obama **I** have appointed him from his birth 'THE

LEADER'S REPRESENTATIVE' as an African to represent **ME THE FATHER GOD ALMIGHTY** and also represent The Messenger of **THE FATHER GOD ALMIGHTY**. Therefore, everybody in the whole universe is required to give their support so that physical PEACE and physical GOOD LIFE can become established on earth. If not so and you refuse to lead a positive life, this world will face such calamities that no generation has ever faced before, but positive children of **THE FATHER GOD** will not have any problems through the NAME and BLOOD of OUR LORD JESUS CHRIST AMEN. So, reconcile with your original first earthly father and mother ADAM and EVE AFRICA NATION and make peace with your soul in order to escape the damnation that will visit the whole world.

G: **THE SPIRITUAL WORLD PEACEMAKERS**

I, THE FATHER GOD constituted this body of **The Spiritual World Peacemakers** today, through this information which **I** have already revealed to HRM King Solomon David **ETE** before today. Do not think that any president can make peace in the world. No spiritualist or any forum of spiritualism or director of any sort can make peace in the world. It is only **I, THE FATHER GOD ALMIGHTY THE CREATOR OF THE UNIVERSE** that can make peace in the entire world because **I** know the **Problem**, the **Cause** and the **Effect**. Nevertheless, **I** can send you to represent **ME** and if you humbly accept this invitation to represent

ME then let all be well with you. But if you refuse and think you can do it by yourself, you will fail woefully and your failure will be the worst of all failures. That is why **I** said earlier in this Lecture Revelation that if President Barack Hussein Obama who represents Africa the fatherland and the motherland, the Original Ancestors, as the **Spirit-Soul** of **STRAINTHEN, THE FATHER GOD'S SPIRIT** that does not want any of **HIS** children in the whole world to suffer, lament and perish fails **ME** then, politics will fail final on earth.

The one to work with Barack Obama in this team is Bill Gates of Microsoft (***HESIGNSTIN***) who is the Disguised Saviour and all the above mentioned personalities. And how did this come about? It came from the **Wisdom Of God, THE FATHER GOD**, who is Solomon and in this present incarnation as HRM King Solomon David Jesse **ETE**. So, **I** have made everything complete. Everything is complete in this arrangement because that is how **I** work.

If however, any of them becomes arrogant and fails the system, then **I** will put them in **oxymoron** area, which is disagreement and declare them wanted souls that will be destroyed forever. Nonetheless, if they carry out the assignments successfully, **I** will use it to forgive the entire world. Then the way forward becomes the BRIGHTNESS FUTURE OF THE SUPREME WORLD. PEACE! PEACE! PEACE of **THE FATHER GOD ALMIGHTY, THE CREATOR OF THE UNIVERSE**!

Obama's Spiritual Assignment

I have already given the instructions on what to do about some of the information contained in this **FATHER'S TALK (GOD PRESENT)** Lecture Revelation. When it is produced **I** have instructed that some information should be blanked or coded. The omitted information will be revealed and decoded physically only when HRM King Solomon David Jesse **ETE'S** presence is requested for in the forum with peace and love.

H: **THE GREAT UNIVERSAL CHANGE**

I have sent out information in **THE FATHER'S TALK (GOD PRESENT)** titled; *THE GREAT UNIVERSAL CHANGE* to the whole world which is published and circulated in book shops everywhere in the world. The book contains other titles including **The Truth About Post Position and Name**, which has to do with behaviours of those that occupy any post and position. And it also contains the Lecture Revelation titled, **The Lovers Of Christ**.

THE GREAT UNIVERSAL CHANGE is the information **I** will use to change the whole world whether you believe it or not. **I** will not repeat that information here but if you want to know about the Lecture Revelations mentioned above, then obtain a copy of the book.

I: **THE SUPREME FUTURE**

THE SUPREME FUTURE is also a title of one of **THE FATHER'S TALK (GOD PRESENT)**

publications and it also circulated in book shops everywhere. If you want, you can obtain the book so that you can know more about the information contained within. It contains the directives for the future world and what will happen in relation to the sort of life that all human beings must live and what **I, THE FATHER GOD** wants in this world. **I** also provided that information as guidance for this mission.

When the presence of HRM King Solomon David Jesse **ETE** is asked for in love and peace, he will present the package of **THE FATHER'S TALK (GOD PRESENT)** publications with these titles *THE SUPREME FUTURE, THE GREAT UNIVERSAL CHANGE, I LOVE YOU, I LOVE YOU TOO, THE UNIVERSAL*

UPDATE, and **HIDU-CUM (THE SUPREME LOVE STORY)** along with this particular Lecture Revelation to President Barack Obama and also to Bill Gates of Microsoft and all the other members of the team.

AO: THE UNIVERSAL SUPREME WORD SEASON CELEBRATION OF THE FATHER GOD AND HIS PEOPLE

This is part of the remedy that will help the whole world to be one and for peace to reign supreme everywhere. And **I** made Bill Gates of Microsoft the co-chairman of this world wide celebration in spirit-soul but it is up to him to physically respond.

THE SUPREME WORD SEASON CELEBRATION, which **I** have revealed to HRM King Solomon **ETE** and He has already started celebrating with His family but **I** wish that the whole world would join Him to recognize, appreciate and honour **ME, THE FATHER GOD, THE SUPREME WORD OF THE UNIVERSE**.

This has nothing to do with politics, religion or any particular groups of people.

It has nothing to with gender, age, status, position or post or any other prescription that human beings like to acquire for themselves.

The **SUPREME WORD CELEBRATION** has everything to do with life, which is **THE WORD, THE FATHER GOD ALMIGHTY**.

I AM not interested in religion or any particular groups of people anymore. **I AM** only interested in LIFE, ONENESS, PEACE, LOVE, HUMILITY, EQUALITY, KINDNESS, MERCY, RIGHTEOUSNESS, JOY, HAPPINESS and GENERAL COOPERATION OF GOODNESS.

And when **I** see the hearts of Obama, Mandela, Yar'Adua, Donald Duke, Godswill Akpabio, and Clarke in South Africa Bill Clinton of America and Neil Kinnock of the UK, they are all positive human beings as **I** have explained earlier but that does not mean that they are perfect. They have small, small negative things that they do in their clubs. **I** know the clubs you all have entered and **I** know every single secret in those clubs and the type of things you all do there and all the 'blah-di-blah' you practice in your clubs particularly the one you call the Presidential Club in disguise! **I** know all that club businesses in this world but **I** overlook them because those clubs are only established here. They were established by evil to link **MY** children to them in the Satan net. However, **I AM** talking about the original nature of these people. Bill Clinton the former American President is a child of **THE FATHER GOD** with humility.

    I know all **MY** children, those who originally came from **ME THE FATHER GOD** and **I** know when Satan lured them into his evil net to enslave them. **I** WILL **DESTROY** THAT EVIL **NET OF SATAN** AND RIP IT INTO PIECES AND COMPLETELY SHRED IT so that the world will have peace.

    Something will happen in this world and all the evil cabinets that they have planted evil practices within to pollute the world with, shall be thrown into the abyss finally and nobody will hear of them again.

I, THE FATHER GOD is here on earth spiritually, in the soul, in the in physical and otherwise doing **MY** work from the time of creation till now and **MY** dwelling home is EVERYWHERE HERE and THERE!

I, THE SUPREME WORD OF THE UNIVERSE is here on earth physically to manifest **MY GLORY** under **HIS *HIGHERISTY*, THE DIVINE MAJESTY THE KING OF KINGS AND THE LORD OF LORDS THE SUPREME WORD OF THE UNIVERSE, GOD PRESENT**. Therefore, it is not just an ordinary human being that **I AM** talking about. **I AM** talking about **HE IS THE FATHER, THE**

CREATOR OF HEAVEN AND EARTH.

This day **that I** give this Revelation, if mankind hears **MY VOICE**, then everything is well for humanity.

The testing of your spiritual blood to know your nature in terms of where you come from is through the program called *THE UNIVERSAL SUPREME WORD SEASON CELEBRATION*.

Every family must celebrate **THE SUPREME WORD** to acknowledge, appreciate and honour **THE SUPREME WORD OF THE UNIVERSE**. That will be the sign to know the positive children of **THE FATHER GOD** and the negative evil children. **I** did this in Heaven and **I** must do it here on earth before the final judgement comes.

In Heaven, **I** ordered all spirits, all souls, all angels to bow down and celebrate **THE SUPREME WORD OF THE UNIVERSE** who is called Christ, but Lucifer objected and said that she would not do that. As she refused she caused herself to become an **oxymoron** spirit-soul. And it is that disagreement and stubbornness that made Lucifer to become the Sent Out spirit-soul till today that is being 'Cast and Banned!' from everywhere here and there forever.

So, if anyone or any soul decides to disagree and be stubborn here on earth, then their soul will be 'cast and banned' and into the Lake of Fire, whether you believe it or not but the choice is yours. You have the choice to believe and accept this program and celebrate **THE SUPREME**

WORD or not to believe and your soul becomes 'Cast and Banned' and banished into the Lake of Fire. This is the final test of blood between **ME THE FATHER GOD** and all human beings.

I want to know those who come from **THE FATHER GOD** as the positive human beings that are Gods that represent the image and likeness of **THE FATHER GOD** but those who come from animals should go back to the "animaldom".

I will bring the final judgement when this information is assimilated. Nobody knows **MY** way! **I AM** the **ONE** that knows what **I** do and **MY** way.

CONCLUSION A:
BARACK OBAMA'S OFFSPRING

When this information is published, this part of the information will not be published but it will remain in the original record.

CONCLUSION A-B
THE SPIRITUAL WORLD PEACEMAKERS

I repeat the names of **The Spiritual World Peacemakers as**:
Nelson Mandela, President Barack Obama, Bill Gate, Clarke of South Africa, Neil Kinnock of United

Kingdom, President Yar'Adua of Nigeria, Governor Godswill Akpabio of Akwa Ibom Nigeria, Donald Duke of Calabar Nigeria, Pastor Justus O Mugbeh of BCS London, Bishop James Ellerbe of BCS USA is one of the copy of David the positive STRAINTHEN, Bishop Tutu of South Africa and Bill Clinton of America. There are so many people that are in this category but **I** mention those that are well tuned to the call. All the people that **I** have mentioned are **The Members of the Spiritual World Peacemakers forerunner.**

From time to time **I** will be upgrading the list, when **I** deem it fit to do that. Bill Clinton of America is part of this, in spirit soul. However, anybody that is not fully positive, **I** will remove such a person from the list and this is what **I** affirm under this part, as the information that came from the sub heading of this Lecture Revelation titled, **Obama's Offspring The Forerunner of Peace**.

I, THE FATHER GOD AM THE CAUSE THE EFFECT AND THE MATTER

I, THE FATHER GOD AM the cause, effect and matter of everything that happens before and after creation. The SPIRIT is unheard, unseen and untouchable but before the SPIRIT can be heard, seen and touched, it must be converted by **MY SUPREME SELF** called **THE POTENCY OF THE SPOKEN WORD**. That is **MY** way of life.

Nobody knows **ME** THE SPIRIT but **I** know **MYSELF**.

You only know **ME, THE FATHER GOD ALMIGHTY** when **MY THOUGHT** of **THE WORD** manifests. Other than that you will NEVER know **THE FATHER GOD ALMIGHTY** so, nobody should claim that they know **ME THE FATHER GOD ALMIGHTY**. You can only know what **I** reveal to you. Just as you only know what **I** reveal to you about **MY** Senior Servant, HRM King Solomon David Jesse **ETE** of whom **I** said was born into Eteroyal Universal Family Ikot-Okwo in Ete Community Ikot Abasi, **Akwa Ibom State,** Nigeria, and Africa. And that, He is the incarnate of the original Abel, the incarnate of the original King Solomon of Israel and the incarnate of King James1 of the United Kingdom. Many,

many other transits are his copies and a notable one is, Haile Selassiei of Ethiopia and all of them have one course which is to make the whole world one. Peace! Peace! Peace!

In this generation **I** have come back! And **WE** must do this thing once and for all, so that humankind shall be saved. This task must be done because it is either all humankind is saved or some stubborn evil ones are destroyed.

Nevertheless, since **I** have come as Our Lord Jesus Christ more than two thousand years ago and saved humankind spiritually by wiping away the sins of humanity with **MY** precious blood, **I** have now come to establish mankind in the correct understanding and wisdom. And that is what **I AM** doing now.

People have said that The Twenty-first Century belongs to Satan. That is a pure lie! ***THE TWENTY-FIRST CENTURY BELONGS TO ME; I AM THAT I AM, THE FATHER GOD ALMIGHTY THE CREATOR OF THE UNIVERSE.*** Moreover, there is nothing like Satan. It is you, human evil that is Satan. If there is lack of love in you then, you are Satan. **I** reiterate that there is nothing like Satan. If you go anywhere at all and asks anyone to please show you Satan, no one would show you Satan therefore you would not see any Satan. But if you go somewhere and see human being with a bad mind, a primitive mind, lacking of love, lacking humility, lacking peace, then you will see the work of

Satan manifesting from that human being. So, show **ME** where you saw Satan, if it is not through hatred, jealousy and all evil activities.

Today is the day that you should know where you stand. If you are positive you are God. If you are negative you are Satan. So, do not allow anybody to deceive you. If you have no understanding you are evil. If you have understanding you are God. Understanding, which is wisdom, means God. Evil is misunderstanding.

You spoil things that **I, THE FATHER GOD** create. You kill a human being that is alive and you call yourself a human being? You are an animal! Even an animal is better than you. All those who come from the tribe of animals and are human-animals will all go back to being animals, finally if they do not take evolution now to improve to positive natures but those who are **MY** true image and likeness will stay on this earth and live peacefully.

Don't try to go and live in the moon. **I** have closed that area. No human being should have hope of going to live in any other planet apart from this earth when you are still a human being. As far as you are born through a woman's womb, this is your very own planet to live. If you try to migrate permanently to another planet, you will never succeed.

I AM THE FATHER GOD OF HEAVEN AND EARTH, THE CREATOR OF THE UNIVERSE. I AM THE ONE GIVING THIS MESSAGE.

DON'T SPEND MONEY TO BUILD ANYTHING IN THE MOON WITH THE HOPE OF GOING TO LIVE THERE OR IN ANY OTHER PLANET. There are beings already occupying these planets.

Let **ME** tell you this, the moon is the celestial home of the **MOTHER GOD**, where all souls are preserved before they are put into a woman's womb as stars of destiny from **ME THE FATHER GOD**.

As for the sun there is no human being that can live there or even go near the sun, not even tens of millions and millions of miles close. Even angels cannot live in the sun. That is **MY Personal Home**. It is from there that **I** fuel the whole universe. Every single life lives from **MY SUPREME ENERGY** that **I** generate from the sun to fuel every human life and the existence of every life. And neither can you go to live in the water physically unless you are dead.

I know that people have been doing all sorts of things and trying to implement all sorts of plans to go and live elsewhere other than the earth plane. At the end of the day what you have done has no meaning. You have only wasted your time! You only prove your arrogance and pomposity because you think you have the carnal knowledge and not perfect wisdom from above. Why don't you have love instead?

The love **I** give in this world, the understanding and wisdom **I** give in this world, is to make everybody on this earth to be happy! All human beings should enjoy free electricity, free water supply, free gas, free road, free transport, free housing and free communication. All these basic amenities should be free! And everybody will be happy to live on this earth. But when you control people and make yourself God and Lord without love and equality for your fellow human being then that means, you are a descendant of Cain therefore you are a wanted soul. **I AM the Cause, the Effect and the Matter** and **I** know everything. Since **I** have decided that human negative endeavours are not the basis and a good reason to live and continue surviving, **I** have come back finally to put things in order and **THE GREAT UNIVERSAL CHANGE** will take effect from the spirit to the soul and from the soul to the physical truth. Things which are not good will not survive but things that are good will survive and live happily and peacefully with **ME, THE FATHER GOD** for eternity, full Stop!

CONCLUSION C: GOD BLESS AMERICA

'GOD Bless America' if America Bless GOD.

GOD will only bless America if America blesses God. If America does not bless **GOD**, why should **I** bless America? Who is America?

America is the son of **THE FATHER GOD**.

America is THE WORD.

America is THE SPIRIT OF WONDER.

When **I** established America, were you there? You who live in America, do you know how America managed to be established as the spoken word?

The original people in America are the ones you call Red Indians from Egypt in Africa originally and what is the meaning of the name Egypt? It means blood. As **I** revealed previously when Abel was killed outside the garden of Eden, that spot where he was killed was named **IYIP** (Egypt), meaning the blood and it is the first place that the original vampire manifested his identity as a killer. And that is why Egypt is the boundary between positive and negative and it is the same Egyptians that are the descendants of India and China in transit separation. There will be full decoded information about this. The people that you call the Red Indians are the people that were been killed in Egypt for sacrifice and rituals. They used to kill them a lot and that is why **I** sent them away from Egypt to other places. **I** sent some of them to Australia as Aborigines and some of them across the Indian Ocean. These are the people you *'quat'* [squat] in a corner because **I** put them in these places to protect those places. So, you must make peace with these people.

Australia must make peace with the Aborigines of Australians. And America must make peace with the Red Indians. Give them equal opportunities as other citizens enjoy. Everybody on earth must enjoy equal opportunity.

ISRAEL FAILED!

ISRAEL can NEVER be called the CHOSEN PEOPLE anymore they can only envy other nation! **I** already left them a long time ago and established the United Kingdom. Then **I** left the United

Kingdom and established America. Nonetheless, the United States of America and the United Kingdom are the Israelites. Who are the ones that **I** call **MY** people? By their fruits ye shall know them.

What are the fruits that show that Israelites are children of **GOD**? Is it fighting? Didn't you hear what Our Lord Jesus Christ said? He said, 'Blessed are the peacemakers for they shall be called Children of **GOD**.' Anybody that would not make peace is not a child of **GOD** but a child of evil and that you should forget about the name and concentrate on the actions. By their fruits ye shall know them!

Who goes about killing people and oppressing, suppressing and taking their lands? What do you do with the land? Why do you have to oppress and suppress people? And after causing trouble you call yourselves children of **GOD**. You most certainly are not children of **GOD** and **I** have never made claim to such people as **MY** children! NO WAY!

Whether you call yourself an Arab, a Jew an African, American, British or any other that you wish to call yourself it really does not matter because everybody is from one Adam and Eve as one father one mother, brotherhood! Peace! If you don't adhere to that then you will be a forgotten stock.

From this present century onwards no nation should go to war with another nation and make innocent people suffer and cry and lament. You spray the blood of people up and down and everywhere. If you have a hand in spilling a single drop of blood by any means whether through instruction or direct action spiritually, soul or physically, you will account for it. You will pay for it for eternity! Do you know that?

Do you know that **I** can forgive you any sin that you have committed but **I** cannot forgive you when you spill blood through killing especially human beings? You are insulting **ME, THE FATHER GOD ALMIGHTY THE SUPREME WORD THE CREATOR OF THE UNIVERSE** because **I AM** LIFE. Do you know how human beings managed to be created? Do you know the meaning of life? Even taking away life through abortion carry severe consequences how much more a physical human being that has been born.

Can you produce water?

Is there any scientist that can make water?

Can any scientist make blood?

Can any scientist make air?

Since you can't make any of these three things, which is the **TRINITY GOD**, then you have no power over any human being. Everybody is liberated in one love. So people should love one another. Co-existence must be the order of the day. Humble yourself before one another. That is all that is required of you, every human being on earth.

You cannot go and command people and kill people anyhow because they are all Gods as long as they are alive and speak the word. What makes you bigger than another person?

As you are an antelope or an elephant that turned to be a

human being, you think you are bigger than a rat that is also an animal and so you consider yourself more important.

Big fish swallow another fish!

Big animal kill a smaller animal!

Big human being suppresses another human being and kills some of them!

What type of business is that? Don't you know that **I, THE FATHER GOD** who created you AM bigger than you and **I** see all your actions? If you give a child a knock on the head wrongly and in the name of slavery or for any type of tyranny, then you are in trouble. So, from today America and the entire nations of the world should sit up straight with the ordinance and fear of **THE FATHER GOD ALMIGHTY**! <u>*Else you will see MY actions in the a way you will not like.*</u>

God Bless America! **I** will Bless America if America Bless **THE FATHER GOD** by representing **ME THE FATHER GOD** in a positive way on earth. LET **MY** PEACE AND BLESSING ABIDE WITH THE ENTIRE WORLD NOW AND FOREVER MORE, Amien!

Obama's Spiritual Assignment

*HRM Queen Solomon David **ETE** thanks **THE FATHER GOD** in Prayer:*

*Let thanks and praises be given to **THE FATHER GOD** in the name of Our Lord Jesus Christ, Amien!*

*Let thanks and praise be given to **THE SUPREME WORD OF THE UNIVERSE** in the blood of Our Lord Jesus Christ. Amen*

Let thanks and praises be given to The Divine Spirit Of Truth, the original STRAINTHEN SPIRIT that has come by HIMSELF to straighten the entire universe, now and forever more. Amen

Holy! Holy! Holy!

*We thank **YOU FATHER**, The Divine Spirit for **THY** love for all thy children and for sending **THY** STRAINTHEN Spirit-soul in all capacities in human form to come and represent **YOU FATHER** to* take away suppression from this earth.

We thank **YOU FATHER** that you have come by thyself to give this Lecture Revelation through which **YOU** have opened the eyes of all **THY** servants whose souls you have given the STRAINTHEN spirit-soul and positive heart to represent thee positively, to take away suppression, evil practices, war, hatred and anything that does not bring glory to thee that makes human beings to be unhappy.

We thank **YOU FATHER** that through this Lecture Revelation you have brought the spirit-soul of liberty to the entire universe. All suppression, all division, all confusion have been taken away by the Divine Spirit of **THYSELF**, the Spirit of Truth.

We thank **YOU FATHER** that your representatives, thy servants through whom **YOU** want to use positively would hear thy WORD and obey so that all will be well with all creations even now and forever more, Amien!

Let thanks and praises be given to **THE FATHER GOD** in the name of Our Lord Jesus Christ, Amien!

Let thanks and praise be given to **THE FATHER GOD** in the blood of Our Lord Jesus Christ. Amen

Let thanks and praises be given to The Impartial, The Love and, The Unity **GOD** who has come to make everything perfectly well for the entire universe, even now and forever more. Amen!

THANK YOU FATHER

Chapter Two

THE SPIRIT OF BILL GATES (BILL GATES AND THE MICROSOFT)

FATHER'S TALK (GOD PRESENT)

Melchizedek, Simon Canaanite **FATHER** Two Thousand and Eight (OC.OB.BOOH) (Wednesday, Third February Year Two Thousand and Eight (03.02.2008)

THE SPIRIT OF BILL GATES

(BILL GATES AND THE MICROSOFT)

Today, it pleases **ME THE FATHER GOD THE CREATOR OF THE UNIVERSE** to bring this Lecture Revelation because this Lecture Revelation is very important. It is to honour King David and Solomon Office Week Celebration Thanksgiving to **ME THE FATHER GOD ALMIGHTY**. The title of this Lecture Revelation is **THE SPIRIT OF BILL GATES**

(BILL GATES AND THE MICROSOFT).
Today, **I** want to reveal a very important thing that people of the whole world do not understand. It is the secret and mystery about **BILL GATES AND MICROSOFT OF UNITED STATES OF AMERICA**.

A: INTRODUCTION

IN THE BEGINNING WAS THE WORD AND THE WORD WAS WITH GOD AND THE WORD IS GOD

As **I** always say, **I, THE FATHER GOD THE CREATOR OF THE UNIVERSE AM THE RECORD MYSELF**. Every single record about life as **Unhearable, unseenable** and **untouchable** is in **ME** but **I** transformed them to become **hear-able, seen-able** and **touchable**. Everything is in **ME THE FATHER GOD**.

And since **I THE FATHER GOD** knows the secrets of **MY** Kingdom, it means that every Secret Record is with **ME**. I can decode the secret about every single individual in this world because **I AM THE SUPREME SPOKEN WORD**, which is everything that is seen in the whole universe. Everything is from **ME** and everything comes back to **ME** and everything is **ME THE FATHER GOD**.

I AM going to reveal the meaning of 'in the beginning was the **WORD** and the **WORD** was with **GOD** and the **WORD** is **GOD**.' And through this **WORD**, everything created was created and without the **WORD**, nothing was created.

And that is why the introduction of this Lecture Revelation is aptly titled: **In the Beginning was the Word and the Word is GOD and that Word is GOD**. When you come across **THE FATHER'S TALK (GOD PRESENT)** Lecture Revelations try to read all of them. Visit THE KING SOLOMON SPIRITUAL LIBRARY, **The Information of GOD, The Infinite Encyclopaedia Of THE FATHER GOD ALMIGHTY, manifested through The Comprehensive And Ability Memory** that **I** have given to His Royal Majesty King Solomon David Jesse **ETE**. It is **Unlimited Boom!** It is **Unlimited Computer**. That is why HRM King Solomon **ETE** is a phenomenon. He is a spiritual and natural Mystic human **GOD**. He is an unknown and a mystique type of human being who represents **THE FATHER GOD** on earth all the time.

Introduction of this Lecture Revelation is also, about how **I THE FATHER GOD** can help you to decode things, understand things and know The Secret of Life.
What is the secret of life? There is no secret of life apart from the **SPOKEN WORD**. Everything you call secret known and unknown is buried in the phrase; **THE WORD**.

The **WORD** is everything. It is **THE TOTALITY OF EVERYTHING**! And that is **I, THE FATHER GOD**. The Servant of **THE FATHER GOD** is the Servant of **THE WORD**. Since His Royal Majesty King Solomon David Jesse **ETE** is The Recorder and the spiritual Keeper of the '***HIGHERCRECIES***' the Secret of

THE UNIVERSAL SUPREME WORD in King Solomon Spiritual Library, **I** have chosen this day which is the Thanksgiving Services of the yearly celebration of King David and Solomon Office on earth to especially earmarked the thanking of **THE FATHER GOD**.

I have given Lecture Revelations titled: *THE MANUAL OF LIFE THE MANUAL OF THE SPOKEN WORD* and *INVESTMENT WITH GOD* **I** have so far given many other Lecture Revelations through which **I** have revealed so many things for the edification of humankind on earth. From time to time **I** will decode some individuals that **I** want to decode whenever it pleases **ME** but today, **I** have decided to reveal who **BILL GATES OF MICROSOFT** actually is to the entire universe. **I**

AM not revealing him because he is rich. And it is not because of his present status or that he is something that has made **ME THE FATHER GOD** to reveal him. **I** want to reveal who he is to the whole world <u>because of whom and what he represents</u>. It is the same way that **I, THE FATHER GOD** have the Record about the Daughter of God, the Queen of England that **I** have about everyone.

Everybody in this world is **MY** child as a son or a daughter and **I** have your records and **I** know whom you represent in the physical world and in the Soul World. **I** therefore advise that you open your mind and use love, mercy and humility to listen to **THE FATHER'S TALK** (**GOD PRESENT**) Lecture Revelation so that you can connect **ME** in spirit to know whether this **WORD** comes from man or from **THE FATHER GOD**.

This is the **WORD** from **THE SUPREME STUDIO OF THE ALMIGHTY FATHER GOD**, broadcasting from the **Mind of Love, Freewill Mind, the Mind of Perfection, and the Unlimited Memory** as **the Cold Room of THE FATHER GOD**, which has nothing to do with any infidel spirit-soul. Abel is a Positive Soul so **I** used his blood to create Solomon and **I** kept Solomon for this assignment.

Solomon was the positive King in Israel who inherited his father, King David's throne. When the place became spoilt, **I** sent him to reincarnate in Western Europe for the first time to form the United Kingdom. He was King James1 of England who compiled the Holy Bible. After this period, Solomon has been coming and going in many ways but this is the first time that **I** have sent Him back on earth to start from where he ended. **I** brought Him to continue to bring out information and bear testimony about **THE HOLY SPIRIT OF TRUTH** through the keeping of The Everlasting Records of **THE FATHER GOD'S WORDS** called **THE FATHER'S TALK (GOD PRESENT)**. And that is why **I AM** using His mouth to reveal this WORD.

Nobody knows the meaning of **BILL GATES AND MICROSOFT**. Even **BILL GATES** may not know himself before now. But after today he will know whom he represents on earth.

B: WHO WAS BILL GATES IN THE FIRST PLACE? WHAT WAS HIS NAME? WHAT TYPE OF SPIRIT-SOUL IS HE FROM?

Since this Lecture Revelation is not going to be long, **I AM** going straight to the point but what connects to **BILL GATES** is too deep to easily be understood by a layman. **I** now want to reveal who **BILL GATES** was before now.

Remember the story of Our Lord Jesus Christ. Our Lord Jesus Christ is the higher Self of Adam as the second Adam incarnate as the Spiritual Adam. And HE is the FATHER of all human races. Our

Lord Jesus Christ was the Second Adam incarnate, the Spiritual Adam. And **I, THE FATHER GOD** was the Christ that came on earth with the Potency of **THE WORD**.

I AM THE WORD and Adam was the house of **THE WORD**. What happened was that the physical body of Adam could not contain **THE WORD** because of the low mentality and the low system therefore, **I** had to use his Higherself of **MYSELF** being **THE WORD** and turn it to be a human being to come into the world in the same house of Adam and call **MYSELF** Our Lord Jesus Christ. And Mary was Eve incarnate but since majority of people know this story **I** will not dwell on it.

When **I** was born, as Jesus on earth, Herod and his group wanted to eliminate the baby

Jesus because they knew that a STAR has come into the world to save HIS people. During that time **I** revealed **MYSELF** to **Four Wise Men** but three of them visited Herod and informed Herod of their mission. Herod thought that as a new King was to be born he was going to take over rulership despite that the coming of Jesus Christ was not to take over the Kingship of Herod because HIS Kingdom was not the physical kingdom. He came to save HIS people but Herod did not know this so he was annoyed and jealous and as a result, he sent his armies to kill all the children so that they would kill the baby Jesus too.

I revealed to the three wise men to inform Joseph and Mary to take **ME** as the baby Jesus to run away to Egypt. On their way to Egypt Satan blocked the road. And you know that Satan is a negative spirit-soul. He knew that **THE LIGHT** was coming to pass through the road as he knew that **THE LIGHT** was coming into the world. As result, he used his armed robbers to block the road however; one of the armed robbers that night was an angel that **I** had planed to be in the raid. He was not an armed robber in nature. He was an angel of **ME** that **I** had kept aside for this assignment. **I** planned before the time. Nothing comes to **THE FATHER GOD** unexpected.

I want to reveal something to you today in that; it is not all the members that you see in your secret society that are your real members. One of your members is

MY angel amongst you to monitor you. He will of-course follow you to do what you do but he will be reporting everything to **ME**. In every situation, **I** have a representative there and that is **MY** secret that **I AM** revealing today. So, don't think that when you sit down anywhere and plan evil, or do any wicked act and any thing that nobody knows and that **I, THE FATHER GOD** do not know. Check all the people there and you will see **ME THE FATHER GOD** amongst you but you may not know and even the person representing **ME** will not know whom he represents.
Nevertheless, **I AM** the Mystery, and **I** represent **MYSELF** in every situation as **THE FATHER GOD**.

As **I** was saying, one of the two thieves on the night that Mary and

Joseph were taking **ME**, the baby Jesus to Egypt was an angel and **I** will mention the name of that angel later on in this Lecture Revelation. That angel was **I**, as the same Jesus Christ but he was an armed robber that had been put in place just to save the situation.

When Joseph and Mary carried **ME**, **I** say **ME** because **I, THE FATHER GOD** was the **ONE**. **I AM** the same SPIRIT talking now. They carried **ME** on their shoulder and were walking towards where the armed robbers had mounted a roadblock. When they reached there, the armed robbers demanded money from them and one of them said that if they did not have money to give them, they would seize the baby. But Mary and Joseph had no money so the same arm robber that said that they would seize the baby said that since they had no money they would kill the baby. **I** in the other thief that was an angel said, 'no I will not accept that. What will be our gain to kill this baby?' The other thief said, 'that is your own business, but this baby is going to die if the parents do not give us any money'. Do you see Satan?

You can only conquer temptation but you can't run away from temptation. So, all children of **GOD** on earth should pray that **THE FATHER GOD** should conquer temptation for you, but do not run away from it because wherever you run to, temptation will follow and come to you but if you face it and pass the test, then you are free form it. And since **I**, **THE FATHER GOD** has passed temptation for **MYSELF**; **I** will pass for all **MY** children, Amen!

So back to Mary and Joseph and **ME** and the two thieves, the satanic thief insisted that he would kill the baby since the baby's parents had no money to give them. The angel thief said to the satanic thief, 'okay let's make a deal. You take all the lootings we made today in exchange for this man and the woman and the baby being left to go'. Alleluia! *Alleluia!*

Alleluia! *Alleluia!*
Alleluia! *Alleluia!*
That was **I, THE FATHER GOD** in that thief therefore it is not every thief that is a thief. That is the reason **I** say that nobody should judge anyone. Leave judgement for **THE FATHER GOD** because it is **I, THE FATHER GOD** alone

that knows the secret of **MY** kingdom.

When the satanic thief saw that his partner, the angel thief had truly handed over all the things they stole that day to him, he agreed that the child should go and that Mary and Joseph should carry their child and go. Then **I** made a promise to the angel thief by speaking through **MY** mother because **I** was just two days old and could not talk physically. So, **I** talked through **MY mama** and said through **MY mama** to the angel thief that 'do not worry, my son will remember you when **HE** will be in the Glory of **HIS FATHER**' and then we departed.

Eventually, these two thieves were apprehended. You know, because they harassed **ME**, **I** allowed that they be arrested but when they were arrested, there was of course business inside. Nonetheless, you shall pay for whatever you sow. When they were arrested that night, they were put in jail and they remained in jail until **I** grew and finished **MY** mission on earth. And eventually they received a death sentence and this death sentence was issued for them on the very day that **I** finished **MY** assignment and wanted to go on the cross. And this was because **I** had to bless that good thief before departure. That was why **I** tallied their death sentence with **MY** crucifixion day.

The good thief was crucified on **MY** right had side and the bad thief on **MY** left hand side. And in order to create a forum for **ME** to bless the good thief, the other one on **MY** left hand side said, 'oga

Jesus, I think you are God, why don't you save yourself and save us from this cross?' **I** did not mind him, because they had to reveal themselves.

Then the good thief said to his partner, '*ah-ah,* you are too insulting. This Holy Man you see, **HE** is really a Holy Man. Did you ever hear that he stole from people? Did you ever hear that **HE** was an armed robber? Did you hear that **HE** did anything evil? They just hanged **HIM** here on the cross because of jealousy, because they don't like the truth. As for us we are armed robbers. We are killers. We deserve this punishment given to us.' Then he turned to **ME** and requested saying 'Lord when you are in your Kingdom remember me in your paradise'!

Then **I** turned **MY** merciful eyes on him and **I** said, "Blessed are those who are merciful for they shall obtain mercy." Since he had mercy on **ME**, because he did his assignment very well, **I** said, "Not when, but today, you will be with **ME** in Paradise. **I** will protect your soul." So he became the first physical man that died and went straight to the Paradise of **GOD** with the cross of **THE FATHER GOD** in his hand. And that is the mystery of the two thieves that were nailed on the same day on the cross with Christ.

How did it happen that they were arrested and held in custody? How did it happen that they were brought out on the same day that Christ was to be crucified and given the same death on the cross? And as they were on the road with Christ that fateful night on their way to Egypt so it happened that the three had to be crucified on the same day. That was why when **I** said that he would be with **ME** in the Paradise of **GOD** through **MY** mother the favour was granted to him that day on the cross. Today is the day **I** want to reveal who that good thief is.

BILL GATES was that good thief on the cross with Christ. He was the man **I** promised that he would be with **ME** in the Paradise of **GOD** because he saved **MY** life. **I** will reveal also why he was able to do that. He did not do that just out of the blue moon rather he was programmed as an angel to come and do that assignment.

C: **WHAT YOU SOW YOU SHALL REAP**

I want to point out first before **I** go further that in this world, whether you believe it or not everything you sow you shall reap. But you will not reap it immediately.

When **I** talked about how people would come back on earth to pay for their bad actions and also those who would come back to enjoy because of their good works, people think that **I AM** joking.

I know what happened and would happen to everybody. One day **I** will reveal who Saddam Hussein is. **I** will reveal everybody if **I** want to. If **I** do not want to reveal any particular individual **I** will not. Just as **I** told you that Cain reincarnated as Absalom, while Abel reincarnated as Solomon and David was their father Adam in the natural way. There is what is called NATURAL PROCESS AND SPIRITUAL PROCESS. Both of them always come but **Natural works for spiritual and the Spiritual helps the Natural**. They are both always around for good reasons. Sometimes they come like angels and sometimes they come like proper human beings. It is the same Absalom that was Judas Iscariot when his father came as the Son of David, the spiritual Adam Our lord Jesus Christ and betrayed HIM and he was Cain who killed his brother Abel.

When a personality of **GOD** comes to this world, he or she must be promoted therefore someone has to broadcast the news. So, most times, evil news brings promotion to positivism. That is what you don't know. **I** will give a full Lecture Revelation about Cain. But today **I AM** telling you, all human beings on earth, that, if you carry a knife to kill people, a gun to kill people, make nuclear weapons, instigate war and go to war and commit any evil at all, they are all the cups you prepare for yourself and all those who support you to drink. Your evil deeds are not for anybody else, but for you and your group to drink eventually.

D: **ANGEL HESIGNSTIN**

HESIGNSTIN is the name of Angel one of **MY MANY SELVES** that was **BILL GATES** at the time of Christ about the incident of the baby Jesus and his parents Mary and Joseph on their way to Egypt. The name of that Angel that was the good and positive thief as **THE SAVIOUR THIEF** is **HESIGNSTIN**.

What are the duties of Angels? Angels are assigned to help the situations that are not signed by **ME THE FATHER GOD**. An Angel is to help those that are oppressed and people that nobody writes home about. They salvage any bad situation to help the situation before it deteriorates because the predicament is not the original plan for the situation.

When Satan wants to do something harmful to anyone or at any place, **I** would use Angels to go and barrier it. **ANGEL HESIGNSTIN** is the Helper of Innocent Souls. It can be a human being and it can be a spirit-soul at the same time, but you would not know. So, the present **BILL GATES OF MICROSOFT** is the Natural Body (House) of that Angel. Nonetheless, that same Angel is now in another form. However, the natural person that was **ANGEL HESIGNSTIN** at the time of Our Lord Jesus Christ was one of the thieves that were crucified on the right hand side of Jesus Christ that was also the same good thief that saved the life of baby Jesus on their way to Egypt. He did not allow his evil partner, the other thief to kill the baby Jesus as his parents were escaping with him to Egypt. That natural person at this present time is **BILL GATES OF MICROSOFT** that has come to reap the promise that **THE FATHER GOD** made to him.

I have told you about the angel that **I** send to help people when they are in trouble. It can be for a single person or family. Just like the Spirit-Soul called **STRAINTHEN** that **I** gave to Nelson Mandela that was the same Spirit-Soul **I** gave to King David Jesse. **I** have revealed all these things.

E: **HE IS TO COME AND HELP THE WORLD NOW**

This **Angel HESIGNSTIN** has come again in this last time as the human being called **BILL GATES**. It does not matter whether he is a holy person or not. Or that he is doing some things that seem bad. Nonetheless, his actual assignment is to establish

MICROSOFT. That Angel itself is now **THE MICROSOFT** operating through **BILL GATES**.

THE MICROSOFT is a Mystic idea that is helping the physical **WORD**. **MICROSOFT** is the PHYSICAL **WORD**, while **THE FATHER GOD HIMSELF** is the SPIRITUAL **WORD**. So the BODY OF THE **WORD** is to help THE SPIRITUAL **WORD**. And it is called **MICROSOFT**. Everything seen in the **MICROSOFT** Computers and everything of its counterparts is THE ANGEL **"HESIGNSTIN"**.

The ENERGY of that Angel called **HESIGNSTIN** is now called **MICROSOFT** operating through **BILL GATES** and all types of Computers on earth. And this angel has a group of family members who are twelve in number and these twelve all work together to improve the systems of humankind on earth. Some of them brought electricity and other aspects of it. Some others brought other scientific and technological inventions of different kinds to elevate the lives of humankind to bring good living in a physical way to represent **THE FATHER GOD THE CREATOR OF THE UNIVERSE**. It is not the work of Satan.

The reason **I** brought this Lecture Revelation is for you to know that anything you do today, you will reap tomorrow. And you cannot do anything without **THE FATHER GOD** sending you. There is more information about **BILL GATES** however, this is up to the point of information **I** allocate to release about him. Moreover, what **I** reveal has covered everything.

MICROSOFT AND BILL GATES is the Angel called **HESIGNSTIN** and He is gaining through the promise of **THE FATHER GOD**. One helped person can help others and the same Angel is trying to help people. If there are people who do not have anything to do and the government cannot help them and nobody in the world does anything about such persons then **MICROSOFT** help them. Microsoft can and has given many people Positive Handwork and nobody can argue about this.

Of all the scientific discoveries and inventions and upon all the things people do and have done, **MICROSOFT** is one of the most positive of all the positive things that **THE FATHER GOD** has established on earth. And whom are these Angels representing in human form? It is **ME, THE FATHER GOD THE CREATOR OF THE UNIVERSE**.

As **I** have revealed this information, a great change will take effect in **BILL GATES** system from now forward to test him because he has to promote **ME, THE FATHER GOD, THE UNIVERSAL SUPREME WORD**, and if he would not do that then '**WE**' will call him back for reassignment, but the work of **MICROSOFT** will still carry on forever. However, the negative part of **MICROSOFT** will be destroyed.

F: **THE THIEF ON THE CROSS**

The Thief on the Cross signifies the sins of the world and the evils of the world. That is what **I** mean by **I**, will destroy the temple and build it three days...' What temple was destroyed? What was destroyed was the human instinct, the carnal instinct that polluted the world. Then the spiritual self came.

Now we are living a **Digital Life in Digital Self**. It is the life that you should love one another, the life that you should not harbour anything evil against somebody, the life that you should protect one another and do everything good for one another.

King Solomon that was Abel and is now HRM King Solomon David

Obama's Spiritual Assignment

Jesse **ETE** is one of **MY POSITIVE SELVES** called "**COMPREHENSIVE AND ABILITY MEMORY**" (*THE WISDOM SELF*) which is the Highest Self of **BILL GATES**. KING SOLOMON SPIRITUAL LIBRARY is THE SUPREME SELF, THE SPIRITUAL HIGHEST SELF of **MICROSOFT** where all Everlasting information is stored and can be processed by **MICROSOFT** because **WISDOM IS THE HIGHERSELF OF KNOWLEDGE**. Now, HRM King Solomon David Jesse **ETE** will physically build what is called **THE WORD CITY**. It is a CITY where **THE WORD** will be processed for eternity. It is the CITY where generations upon generations will know that there is a particularly city built and kept for **THE WORD** as **THE WORD CITY**. And this **WORD**

PROCESSING CITY will be the **PHYSICAL WORD** while **BILL GATES** already has the **DIGITAL WORD** as **MICROSOFT** that is used in processing the physical **WORD**.

HRM King Solomon David Jesse **ETE** has also inherited the directives on how to appreciate **THE WORD**. He will lead the whole world to appreciate **THE SUPREME WORD** as the first appreciator. **I** have previously said this.

All the people **I** have revealed through the WORD now will join hands to build what is called **THE SUPREME MERCY SHRINE** for **THE WORD** to honour **THE SUPREME WORD ON EARTH– THE KING OF KINGS AND THE LORD OF LORDS**.

I AM now revealing that **MICROSOFT** should sponsor **THE WORD** just as it happened last time. If he fails this then he will fail forever. So, if you know **BILL GATES** and have ways of reaching him, make sure that before his days are finished on earth, he has access to this revelation. So, the two thieves on the cross with Christ represent positivism and negativism spiritually. **I** do not want to talk about the evil thief that was representing Satan now.

Human beings cannot avoid committing sins. And since human beings cannot avoid sinning **I** kept THE SUPREME ENERGY OF THE BLOOD OF JESUS CHRIST as a way for forgiving sins. And any day you say "**FATHER** FORGIVE ME" **I** will forgive you, but you must forgive one another also.

Everybody is shouting that **BILL GATES** is a philanthropist doing lots of charity. He has not done enough! What **BILL GATES** has belongs to **THE FATHER GOD** because **I, THE FATHER GOD** sent him to come and help everybody particularly poor people and honour **ME THE UNIVERSAL SUPREME WORD OF GOD**.

BILL GATES does not have the awareness of himself within this direction yet. He thinks he is the one that is so wealthy. He does not know who he is however from today that **I** have revealed him changes shall take effect in him for good.

G: **EVERY RECORD OF HUMANKIND IS WITH ME THE FATHER GOD ALMIGHTY**

This shows that **I, THE FATHER GOD** have records of everybody. If you come closer to **ME, I** will decode your record one after another.
I have assigned SEVENTY-TWO MILLION RECORDS to be revealed in KING SOLOMON SPIRITUAL LIBRARY. It does not matter the time and generation. **I** will do **MY WILL**. The time shall come that any information you want will be found in KING SOLOMON SPIRITUAL LIBRARY which is also called THE INFINITE BOOM! UNLIMITED RECORD. So, as much as anybody on earth shall support it, such a person has revealed

himself or herself as a positive child of **GOD**, of the offspring of Abel. If you are not positive, you cannot accept this information and so cannot support it. That is what **THE FATHER GOD** has revealed today.

Records of All Humankind Are with ME THE FATHER GOD, and are hiding in KING SOLOMON SPIRITUAL LIBRARY. That is **THE SUPREME MEMORY OF THE FATHER GOD** as **THE FATHER GOD'S** CENTRAL INFORMATION.

When **I** reveal things and tell people, they don't believe **ME**, but as far as this **RECORD** is concerned, you will know in time to come. The convincer will convince you whether you believe it or not.

CONCLUSION A:
DO GOOD AND GOOD WILL FOLLOW YOU

This is the reason **I** say that everybody should think well, speak well, hear well, see well and do well. If you do good, good will follow you. This Lecture Revelation about **BILL GATES** is a glaring example of that.

There is nobody that does good things and those good things would not follow such a person. Because when you do any good thing the action is recorded and put in the Memory of **THE FATHER GOD** and it will stay there forever therefore it must surely come back to you.

When your name and your original nature that represents your assignment and what you stand for is called, all your good deeds that are kept under that will be brought forward for your next coming so that you can enjoy the fruits of your good deeds.

Nobody can tell **ME** that **BILL GATES** is not enjoying life now. Nobody can tell **ME** that **BILL GATES** can go to join armed robbery and rob people. Nobody can tell **ME** that **BILL GATES** is not helping people now.

BILL GATES was the angel **HESIGNSTIN**, but that angel now is no more a human being. Nonetheless, he is still doing the work of an angel, but he works through **BILL GATES** just as **I**, **THE FATHER GOD** is talking through HRM King Solomon **ETE** now.

Every human being on earth stands for something. All your inspirations mean the spirits-souls that are supporting you and that means that they are behind you to achieve. Nonetheless, **BILL GATES** knows himself that he is no ordinary human being.
Do Bad, Bad Will Follow You. Do Good, Good Will Follow you, wherever you go.

CONCLUSION B:
THERE IS TIME FOR EVERYTHING

King Solomon said in Ecclesiastes that there is a time for everything under the sun.
Today! Is the day that **I, THE FATHER GOD** have set aside to reveal this information to show you that humankind do not know

the sources of riches? Some people can kill to be rich, but that holy thief was originally not a member of any evil group. It was the same day of the incident described earlier that his evil thief friend invited him to join them because he requested some help from him since he was very poor and he did not have food to eat for three days. His parents were both dead and there was no one to help him. It was due to the situation that **I, THE FATHER GOD** had put him through, that led him to fulfil his spiritual assignment by joining the other thief that very night because that is how **I, THE FATHER GOD, THE SUPREME SPIRIT OF ALL THINGS OPERATES** to fulfil **MY WILL**.

Some people can do all sorts of things to be rich and would think that the things they do are the reason they are rich but they do not know the actual cause of their riches are beyond their knowledge.

If you think killing to be rich makes one rich then **I** can tell you that many people have killed to be rich and yet they are not rich. If you think people engaged in armed robbery get rich then ask you how many people are armed robbers and go out with arms to steal and are killed that same day? Anything you do in this world and succeed means that GOD'S signature is there. Without that you cannot succeed. Go and read the Lecture Revelation titled **THE SIGNATURE OF GOD**.

Today, **I** have revealed to you that there is a time for everything under the earth. There is the time that you sow and the time that you reap.

The time that you sow is the time that you are not happy. But the time when you reap, if it is positive is when you will enjoy. If it is negative then that is when you will cry. This is straightforward information for all humankind.

CONCLUSION C:
THIS IS THE TIME OF REVELATIONS

I said that this Lecture Revelation is a short one, but it is a very important Lecture Revelation. It is an exemplary Lecture Revelation to all the people that have the opportunity to do good things, to think well, to speak well, to hear well, to see well and to do well but refuse to do good things. If that is the case then you have taken voluntary evolution to deprive yourself of good things, just as the other thief on the left side of the cross of Christ deprived himself. That is called Double Thief. Double thief does not need forgiveness.

If you have stood the chance to show mercy, but you refused to take the chance then you would have no mercy because you have forfeited mercy for yourself. You stood the chance to have love yet you could not love then there is no love for you. You must do whatever good things you want from others to others.

How can somebody steal from a fellow thief? Two people went and stole something, but kept what they stole at close quarters to each other. **I** will now tell you the story of thief, thief and thief. That is, thief stole from a fellow thief.

There were two thieves that went about stealing things because of the difficult condition that they found themselves. These two thieves were two women. They had nothing to eat and so they decided to go to a farm that belonged to someone else and steal some food. The person in question whose farm they went to was a very rich woman.
The aim of these women was just to go and take a little thing they would eat for a while and not to finish everything in the farm. That

is, they would not uproot all the cassava in the rich woman's farm.

When they have concluded on what to do and how to go about it, they decided that since they were not going to uproot all the cassava in the farm, they would each take a basin full of cassava. One thief carried just one basin but the other carried two basins, unbeknown to her fellow thief. She had put another basin inside the one she carried.

So, when they got to the farm they planned to steal cassava from, they embarked on the business of the day. When they each filled up their basins with the cassava, the one with one basin said she needed to relieve herself before they started going back home. She went further into the forest to relieve herself.

While she was far away into the bush, the other thief stole the cassava from her basin and filled her other basin and went and hid it somewhere so that the woman would not see that she had two basins full of cassava however it was only two of them in the farm. You know evil people do not think well. They don't think well at all.

When the one that went to relieve herself came back, a considerable portion of cassava had disappeared from her basin. She asked her fellow thief saying 'my dear what happened to my cassava in my basin'? The guilty one answered, 'I don't know oh! Should I have protected your cassava for you? Did you pay me to protect your cassava?' The other said, 'but it is only the two of us that are here. If you wanted to steal more, you should do it well and not steal again from the ones I stole. Did we not agree that we are doing this because we had nothing to eat? And now look at what you have done. Your own 'thieving' is very bad. Your kind of stealing is thief, thief from thief'. At this point, they started fighting.

They fought and fought and fought. Then the double thief took something and hit the other one real hard and she fell on the ground lifeless, but did not actually die. However, she panicked and started shouting and shouting so people came. They asked what happened. She said that someone came and attacked them and beat them mercilessly and killed her friend and that she managed to survive the ordeal thinking that the other woman had died. The woman that fell to the ground got up and said, "*na lie!*"

She told those that gathered that this woman is a thief, a proper thief, a double thief. She then reported what had actually happened. The thief-thief was then arrested and put in prison, where she stayed for a long, long time and finally died there in the prison. The other woman was pardoned and set free.

So, you that is thief-thief that went and stole once and had what to help yourself with, why don't you stop. You continue to go and steal and steal and yet some more. You will not get any mercy from **ME THE FATHER GOD**. You are a prostitute and you have done prostitution for so long and become a proper prostitute, because now it is a sweet thing for you to do. But initially, you went into prostitution because of a difficult condition and **THE FATHER GOD** forgave you. You now carried on with prostitution because of the easy money and because you enjoy doing it so much so you have become an evil prostitute. You will not obtain forgiveness again.

If you do any bad thing intentionally, **I THE FATHER GOD** will not forgive you. Therefore, **I AM** giving you this Lecture Revelation so that you will know these things. **THIS IS THE TIME OF REVELATIONS**.

THIS IS THE TIME OF REVELATIONS! TRUE REVELATIONS! Positive Revelations! TRUTH has come to stay. THE WORD OF GOD HAS

COME TO LIFE. **I** know everything that is going on, but don't be thief-thief-thief. Double sin is the sin that you have no repentance.

But look at that Angel, that saviour! Everybody is happy that Jesus died. Jesus died for humankind! Jesus died for humankind everybody shouts! Apart from being Jesus, whomever that would have behaved in any such circumstances like that good and holy thief to save any human being deserves to be blessed.

What is it that **BILL GATES** is doing today to have such riches at his disposal? A simple thing like Microsoft, a simple thing like processing the **WORD**, a simple thing like having an instrument that puts words together, a simple thing with digital manipulation has become the number one thing in the whole world as a positive investment.

In a similar manner, a simple thing like appreciating **THE FATHER GOD** in the Garden of Eden yielded huge blessings for the first Chief Appreciator, ABEL, as HIS ROYAL MAJESTY KING SOLOMON DAVID JESSE **ETE**.

I used the **WORD** to create Adam and Eve in the Garden of Eden. **I** used the **WORD** to create everything! But no single person appreciated that! Nobody appreciated **ME**. Even Adam did not appreciate **ME**, until Abel decided that he should appreciate **THE FATHER GOD** for the wonderful work **THE FATHER GOD** had done. From that day till tomorrow, Abel is the Chief

Appreciator of **THE FATHER GOD, THE UNIVERSAL SUPREME WORD**.

The reason **I** did not call him Abel again was because **I** elevated his spirit in the new construction called **Second Thought of GOD** and made him King Solomon to secure his soul. THE WONDERFUL MAGIC POWER OF SOLOMON IN HIS NAME IS THE '3**O**s' IN-BETWEEN S-L-M-N because, that is **ME, THE FATHER GOD ALMIGHTY** INDWELLING IN HIM FOREVER. And because of that **I** promised that the blessing **I** give to him **I** would not give to anybody else. That is **ME MYSELF**, and **MY** SUPREME SECURITY!

LET **MY** PEACE AND BLESSING ABIDE WITH THE ENTIRE WORLD, NOW AND FOREVER MORE. Amen.

Next time **I** will reveal something about Michael Jackson and the rest of people like that.

THANK YOU FATHER!

Prayer by Queen Disem Solomon David **ETE**

*Let thanks and praises be given to **THE FATHER GOD** in the name of Our Lord Jesus Christ. Amen*
*Let thanks and praises be given to **THE FATHER GOD** in the blood of Our Lord Jesus Christ. Amen*
*Let thanks and praises be given to **THE ALMIGHTY FATHER GOD THE CREATOR OF THE UNIVERSE, THE SUPREME RECORD, THE ONE WHO HAS THE RECORDS OF EVERYTHING** heard and unheard, seen and unseen, touchable and untouchable and the entire universe, even now and forever more. Amen.*
Holy! Holy! Holy!
*Thank You **FATHER GOD** for this Lecture Revelation about Bill Gates and about Microsoft and the*

*Word. And also thank YOU **FATHER** for ability to comprehend this information. Thank YOU **FATHER** for revealing that Microsoft is YOUR own WORD in the physical form and that this WORD has to come to appreciate **THE SUPREME WORD.**
(FATHER GOD cut in: **HE IS THE WORD HIMSELF)**
Thank YOU **FATHER** that you are **THE SUPREME APPRECIATION** and you have given the ability for Bill Gates **THY** own angel, **THY** divine Angel whom **YOU** created for this purpose to come and appreciate what he has benefited from. And for all children of **GOD** to appreciate and benefit from what he has benefited so that we will all benefit from **YOU** the original source of everything, now and forever more. Amen*

*Let thanks and praises be given to **THE FATHER GOD** in the name of Our Lord Jesus Christ. Amen*
*Let thanks and praises be given to **THE FATHER GOD** in the blood of Our Lord Jesus Christ. Amen*
*Let thanks and praises be given to the **Source** and **Destination** of everything and through whom everything manifests, now and forever more. Amen.*

THANK YOU FATHER

Chapter Three

THE VOICE OF THE CREATOR OF THE UNIVERSE

FATHER'S TALK
(GOD PRESENT)
Enoch, Sixteenth James, FATHER Two Thousand and Eight (AF.OF.OH) (Monday, Sixteenth June, Year Two Thousand and Eight (16.06.2008))

In the Name of Our Lord Jesus Christ, In the Blood of Our Lord Jesus Christ, Now and forever more

THE VOICE OF THE CREATOR OF THE UNIVERSE THE FATHER GOD ALMIGHTY TO ALL HUMAN BEINGS ON EARTH

This is the **VOICE OF THE CREATOR OF THE UNIVERSE THE FATHER GOD ALMIGHTY** to all human beings on earth. ***This is the final information and the last remedy to solve the universal Problems of mankind: natural disasters, sickness, and conflicts, wars between nations, disagreements, reporting of many incidents of death and general destruction on earth***.

A: **I, THE FATHER GOD THE CREATOR OF THE UNIVERSE** deserve recognition and total acknowledgement as **THE SUPREME FATHER** who creates and owns all spirits, souls, angels, humans and everything created seen and unseen

B: All **MY** creations should have the total belief in **ME THE SUPREME FATHER GOD THE CREATOR OF THE UNIVERSE**, and refrain completely from worshipping of idols, elementary spirits of any kind, practicing wickedness of any form, and you have to disassociate yourself completely from any negativism and incantations.

C: Everyone should join His Royal Majesty King Solomon David Jesse ETE, the original

incarnate of Abel, the positive son of Adam and Eve to celebrate and appreciate **ME, THE SUPREME FATHER GOD ALMIGHTY**, through the universal programme of the **UNIVERSAL SUPREME WORD SEASON CELEBRATION**, which is a yearly event.
I AM THE UNIVERSAL SUPREME WORD, the **MOTIVATOR** of **LIFE** and **LIGHT** of **LIFE SUPREME ENERG**Y. Therefore, any living soul that rejected this order has himself or herself to blame because of the universal testing programme that **I AM** going to start, in spirit, soul and physical, to shake the

world, to remove all shakeable things away, and then all the positive things shall remain on earth.

It has pleased **ME, THE FATHER GOD THE CREATOR OF THE UNIVERSE** to have long patience, longest of all long patience and up till this time. All human beings, all the kings and Queens, Heads of States, Presidents, Governors, daughters and sons of all human beings give deaf ears to **ME** and **MY WORD OF LOVE**, and all the preaching **I** have been passing through **MY** positive Servants to delivered. They still treat the world as though it belongs to them – with total power of evil, still maintain that there is nothing like **THE FATHER GOD THE OWNER OF THE UNIVERSE**. The whole world has refused to acknowledge **MY** presence as the **SUPREME WORD, THE SUPREME SPIRIT**, and the Owner of ALL things. They rather worship negativism. They worship mermaids and elementary spirits soul instead of their **CREATOR**. **I** have no other option than to exercise **MY** Ownership on earth in whatsoever form **I** like from now on.

So, what human beings will see on earth from now onwards, starting from a very limited time and nobody should predict time for **ME**, they should not doubt. Nobody knows **MY** will. **I** will do what **I** want and select the positive and destroy all negatives in spirit, soul and physical present. Therefore, in spirit and in soul, if you give deaf ear to this information then, **I** repeat! You have yourself to blame and your soul and your blood will be upon you.

I do everything to salvage mankind and to save your soul, because **I** know the problem you will face if your soul falls into darkness hell. It is so severe. Everlasting punishment is so severe, which **I** do not wish any of **MY**

creations to face. That is why being that **I AM LOVE, I** always bring remedy to mankind in the time like this on earth. So, this is the last and the final remedy, **THE VOICE OF THE CREATOR** to you all **MY** creations.
What was done in Heaven should be done on earth, which was the pleading of the higher positive spirit soul of Adam, which is our Lord Jesus Christ that, what happened in Heaven should also occur here on earth. So, now this is what will happen here on earth: Every soul, every human being will join to celebrate ***THE UNIVERSAL SUPREME WORD SEASON*** and recognize **THE FATHER GOD** in all aspects of life and shun all negativism. Without

that well...! This is your last chance.

THE UNIVERSAL SUPREME WORD SEASON CELEBRATION

covers the following celebration criteria and appreciations –

A: Celebrate and appreciate **THE FATHER GOD THE CREATOR OF THE UNIVERSE**

B: Celebrate and appreciate the first human beings Adam and Eve, our first father and mother, the universal Parents of all human beings (BROTHERHOOD) on earth

C: Celebrate and appreciate the positive life – our lives on earth.

D: Celebrate and appreciate **THE FATHER GOD** The divine

breathe of life in you – your personal life.

E: Celebrate and appreciate **THE FATHER GOD** the soul of life in you – your personal soul.

F: Celebrate and appreciate **THE FATHER GOD** for sound health – your human physical presence here on earth.

G: Celebrate and appreciate **THE FATHER GOD** for **HIS** love, peace, mercy, kindness, equality, goodwill, righteousness, joy and happiness, long life and prosperity and the rest of all **HIS** good countless goodness for mankind.

H: Celebrate and appreciate **THE FATHER GOD** for **HIS**

positive **DIVINE SELF, THE HOLY SPIRIT OF TRUTH, HE** is the **SPIRIT** of all things **BROTHERHOOD**

I: Celebrate and appreciate **THE FATHER GOD, HIS** Divine positive soul. **HE** is the **WORD**, the Supreme Word of the Universe.

AO: Celebrate and appreciate **THE FATHER GOD**, for **HIS** Positive Divine Power, the Holy Spirit of Truth personified on Earth.

THE CELEBRANT-
EVERY HUMAN BEING IS A CELEBRANT
The above are the reasons that every human being is a celebrant of ***THE UNIVERSAL SUPREME WORD SEASON CELEBRATION***.

Therefore, it is a must and compulsory that every living soul, especially human kind to do this programme with all their heart. This is the only way **I, THE FATHER GOD THE UNIVERSAL SUPREME WORD, THE CREATOR OF THE UNIVERSE** will give you credit that you recognize **MY EXISTENT AS THE FATHER GOD ALMIGHTY YOUR CREATOR**.
Nevertheless, this can only be done if you love one another and appreciate another life like life in you. Also you appreciate **ME THE FATHER GOD, THE SUPREME WORD** that lives in every soul by respecting and value another life, all live and all living creatures.

Let my peace and blessing abide with the entire world, now and forever more. Amen.

In the Name of Our Lord Jesus Christ, In the Blood of Our Lord Jesus Christ, Now and forever more

THANK YOU FATHER.

PART FOUR

THE INSPIRATIONAL WRITER

KING SOLOMON SPIRITUAL LIBRARY

THE GOD ENCYCLOPAEDIA WORD OF INFINITY

INSPIRATIONAL WRITERS AND READERS OF THE FATHER'S TALK

(GOD PRESENT)

KING SOLOMON SPIRITUAL LIBRARY

In the name of our Lord Jesus Christ, In the blood of our Lord Jesus Christ, Now and forever more, Amien

(A) REFERENCING THE FATHER'S TALK (GOD PRESENT) IN KING SOLOMON SPIRITUAL LIBRARY

I know that some people will be inspired when they visit King Solomon Spiritual Library website or bookshop, and have access to any of **THE FATHER'S TALK (GOD PRESENT)** information through books, electronics, audio and otherwise and are inspired to write or produce any information through the knowledge that they have gained, they must not fail to reference **THE FATHER'S TALK (GOD PRESENT)** in **King**

Solomon Spiritual Library as the source of your inspirations.

(B) THE WORD OF TRUTH AND THE HOLY SPIRIT PRINCIPLES

Since **THE FATHER'S TALK (GOD PRESENT)** is the direct information from **I THE FATHER GOD ALMIGHTY HIMSELF**, all positive children of **GOD** can be, and will be inspired with this **WORD** because the **WORD** of **THE FATHER GOD, THE CREATOR OF THE UNIVERSE** is a Spiritual Case Study for all souls to improve to have self awareness and a Higherself Consciousness.

When you are inspired and you want to write, make sure that your ideas, principles and concepts are based on the Holy

Spirit of Truth without changing the ordinance of the **FATHER'S TALK (GOD PRESENT)**.

(C) THERE SHALL BE CONSEQUENCES THAT WOULD FOLLOW THOSE WHO USE THE MEANING, THE CONCEPTS AND THE PRINCIPLES OF THE FATHER'S TALK (GOD PRESENT) FOR THE PURPOSES OF MISLEADING

Consequences shall follow those who use the meaning, the concepts and the principles of **THE FATHER'S TALK (GOD PRESENT)** for the purposes of misleading in any manner.

Any Human-God, human-animal, human-bird or human-fish who has access to **THE FATHER'S TALK (GOD PRESENT)** through any means, be it via books, electronics, audio and otherwise should know that those words are not the words of human beings. The words are transcribed, proofread and accepted by **ME THE FATHER GOD** as it comes from the **SUPREME STUDIO OF THE ALMIGHTY FATHER GOD HIMSELF**, via **King Solomon Spiritual Library**.

When the signal of the information alerts HRM King Solomon David Jesse **ETE** from **I THE FATHER** through the **COMPREHENSIVE MEMORY OF GOD** in Him, at anytime in the day or at night and anywhere, whether on the road or any public place, he will take note of the title of the Revelation Lectures. Sometimes if the location is conducive, lectures can take place immediately. If the location is not conducive, **I THE FATHER GOD** fixes the time for the full Lecture Revelation to take place. Most of the time, some of the Lecture Revelations take about a week, a month or six months and so on, to deliver when **I THE FATHER GOD** brings it back from **HIS SUPREME MEMORY** to HRM King Solomon **ETE**.

Take note that the information of **THE FATHER'S TALK** (**GOD PRESENT**) is not preaching, or the giving of sermons or shared discussion. **THE FATHER GOD** calls them "***LECTURE REVELATIONS***", which is a Spiritual Case Study for humankind to improve and have the Higherself Consciousness about himself or herself and their **CREATOR**.

For this reason, every human being that comes across any of the information of the **FATHER'S TALK** (**GOD PRESENT**) should treat it with utmost and absolute respect and reverence at all times.

HRM King Solomon David Jesse **ETE** is not responsible for **THE FATHER'S TALK** (**GOD PRESENT**) but **ME, THE FATHER GOD HIMSELF. I, THE ALMIGHTY FATHER** only use Him as a way through, just like a loud speaker from the radio or television receiver.

For this reason, HRM King Solomon David Jesse **ETE** will not be held responsible by anyone who does not understand the contents, the concepts and the principles of **THE FATHER'S TALK**

(**GOD PRESENT**) information in King Solomon Spiritual Library. He will not answer any questions or queries from spirit to soul and the physical truth in connection to the above from the lower mind individuals, persons or groups. However, if you are positive and you have love and are humble, have patience and are peaceful and you want to know and understand more of any part of **THE FATHER'S TALK (GOD PRESENT)**; '**You should use fasting and prayer**' and or if anyone has any questions in good faith, he or she is free to write to HRM King Solomon and **THE FATHER** in him will respond. He will not, and there is no response to any questions, queries and anything negative with the craftiness of the evil minds of humankind.

That is why you should first read seven **FATHER'S TALK (GOD PRESENT)** Lecture Revelations before commenting and

THE FATHER GOD with **HIS SUPREME HOLY SPIRIT OF TRUTH** will bless all those who read and accept this information with good faith through the name and blood of our Lord Jesus Christ, *Amien*.

In the name of our Lord Jesus Christ In the blood of our Lord Jesus Christ Now and forever more, Amen

ESTABLISH MY SPIRITUAL LIBRARY

I THE FATHER GOD ALMIGHTY THE SUPREME WORD OF THE UNIVERSE AM THE SPIRITUAL FOOD TO FEED YOUR SOUL. Therefore, **I** want every family in this world, every home in this world, every office, government offices, monarchies, countries, states, regions, counties, communities, local authority compounds, family homes and everyone and everywhere to collect published copies of **THE EVERLASTING GOSPEL AND THE FATHER'S TALK (GOD PRESENT)** Lecture Revelations of KING SOLOMON SPIRITUAL LIBRARY and establish it physically in your houses. This is so that everybody would have these RECORDS. Go to read the books regularly. Every family should have a Library of **MY INFORMATION CENTRE** for their family members.

Every generation of a particular family should be able to easily go to their family Library of KING SOLOMON SPIRITUAL LIBRARY EVERLASTING GOSPEL and the **FATHER'S TALK (GOD PRESENT) Lecture Revelations** and read the Gospels and Lecture Revelations so that generations upon generations will access their KING SOLOMON SPIRITUAL LIBRARY.

You must all have **THE LIBRARY OF THE FATHER GOD ALMIGHTY** called **KING SOLOMON SPIRITUAL LIBRARY THE FATHER'S TALK (GOD PRESENT) LECTURE REVELATIONS** in your homes and offices. The authorities and individuals concerned must see to that. When you establish your branch of KING SOLOMON SPIRITUAL LIBRARY and have the **EVERLASTING GOSPELS** and the **FATHER'S TALK (GOD PRESENT)** Lecture Revelations then that place is blessed and secured. In the name and Blood of Our Lord Jesus Christ, now and forever more, *Amien*.

THANK YOU FATHER

"THEUNISAL-SUREME SEACELION"
The Universal Supreme Season Celebration

=========

"THEUNI-SUREME WORA THECRO-THEUNISE"
The Universal Supreme Word Almighty
The Creator Of The Universe

==================

WWW.COME4WORD.COM

THE OFFICIAL SITE FOR

==============

EVERLASTING

Obama's Spiritual Assignment

UNIVERSAL ALL WORD SEASON APPRECIATION CEREMONIAL PROGRAM

========

==

THE UNIVERSAL SUPREME

ALL WORD SEASON CELEBRATION (GOD PRESENT) SOMETHING MORE THAN 'GOLD'

Obama's Spiritual Assignment

THE HEART OF ALL MEN IS

WORD

==================

THE WORD IS THE MAKER, THE SOLE ADMINISTRATOR AND THE CREATOR OF THE UNIVERSE THEREFORE, ALL HUMANKIND ON EARTH MUST APPRECIATE THE WORD IN ALL CAPACITIES FOREVER

===============

FROM EVERY OA OF AO TO AO OF AO (1st OCTOBER TO 10th OCTOBER). YEARLY IS THE UNIVERSAL SUPREME

ALL WORD SEASON

CELEBRATION TO APPRECIATE THE FATHER GOD ALMIGHTY

==================

CELEBRATION! CELEBRATION!!

CELEBRATION !!! THE UNIVERSAL SUPREME WORD CELEBRATION OF ALL TIME
=======

Obama's Spiritual Assignment

THE ALMIGHTY FATHER GOD, THE CREATOR OF ALL THINGS BROTHERHOOD

ORGANISED BY
KING SOLOMON SPIRITUAL LIBRARY
=======
HRM KING SOLOMON DAVID JESSE ETE
INSPIRATIONAL HEAD

IN THE HONOUR OF THE FATHER GOD THE CREATOR OF THE UNIVERSE
THE HOLY SPIRIT OF TRUTH
AND THE KING OF KINGS AND THE LORD OF LORDS
==========
THANK YOU FATHER

KING SOLOMON SPIRITUAL LIBRARY

THE GOD ENCYCLOPAEDIA WORD OF INFINITY

=============

King Solomon Spiritual Library, God Universal Information Centre
FATHER'S TALK (GOD PRESENT)

WITH LOVE

Covered: This BOOK, e-book, software or software's, books, websites, videos, audios, idea or ideas, formula or formulas, manual or instruction manual

... Hereby gives you a non-exclusive license to use the ... (THIS BOOK).

Some of the words here are coded with the (WORD OF SUPER HOLY AND INTELLIGENCE FATHER GOD ALMIGHTY)

Title, ownership rights, and intellectual property rights in and to the Website, Books, E-book, Audios and Videos, Shops and Store – e-Stores, Fundraisings, Celebrations and the Supreme Word Seasons Celebration formulas and arrangements, Positive Inspiration, HOLY (FATA), FATHER GOD ALMIGHTY POSSESSING SPIRIT in thought, in words and in deed, thinking well, speaking well, hearing well and doing well shall remain in me and in ... The BOOK is protected by international copyright.

FATHER'S TALK (GOD PRESENT)

The message in **THE FATHER'S TALK (GOD PRESENT)** does not challenge any authority as individuals, groups or governments of any land or even any belief of any form. It is rather challenging the truth that is hidden from mankind. Therefore, any spirit, soul or physical human being who decides to challenge this truth shall have himself or herself to blame.

Key A: Any individual that reads any of **THE FATHER'S TALK (GOD PRESENT)** with faith; love and acceptance will experience immediate positive change in his or her life from spirit, soul to physical. If he or she accepts the message then he or she will be free from any evil.

Key B: **PEACE AND LOVE**
If you do not believe the contents of any of **THE FATHER'S TALK (GOD PRESENT),** it is possible through **THE FATHER'S** divine love and peace to simply hand over your copy to a friend or somebody else that would like to keep a copy, or by signing out from any of the websites that connect to **THE FATHER'S TALK (GOD PRESENT)** and KING SOLOMON SPIRITUAL e-LIBRARY without any evil and negative comments then you are blessed and free.

FROM THE DESK OF THE INSPIRATIONAL HEAD

Fees, Prices and Donations; There is no refund on fees, prices or donations since your fees, priced payments or donations are used as a charity contribution to do administrative work of **THE SUPREME WORD**, so please kindly read this first before you decide to involve yourself in any of the under mentioned of HRM King Solomon David Jesse **ETE** universal Inspirational Businesses of (**GOD PRESENT**) in cash, kind and otherwise.

I CAME FROM THE FATHER GOD, WITH THE FATHER GOD, AND BY THE FATHER GOD TO ESTABLISH THE FOLLOWING:

THE FATHER'S TALK (GOD PRESENT), The Spiritual Advice, Healing and Counselling on General Live (The Universal

Supreme Spiritual General Hospital), New Songs and Psalms of King David and Solomon, The Word of **GOD** Processing City in Ikot Okwo or e-City online, The Trinity Celebration, "**OUC FUND**", The Universal Bank Account For All Creations, "**ERUFA**" ETE Royal Universal Family, "**THEUNISAL-SUREME SEACELION**" The Universal Supreme Word Season Celebration To Appreciate **THE FATHER GOD ALMIGHTY "THEUNI-SUREME WORA THECRO-THEUNISE" The Universal Supreme Word Almighty, THE CREATOR OF THE UNIVERSE. Therefore** all distributors and contributors should attach and make this information available to all readers, website visitors, distributors, affiliates person/group, celebrant and celebrations centres, supporters and promoters, members, workers and voluntary workers, Ete royal universal palace committee, governments and many other centres as an agreement. Please kindly know that I am not answering to any physical human except **PEACE, UNITY AND LOVE.**

"THEUNISAL-SUREME WORA THECRO-THEUNISE".

I AM IN THE STAGE OF SUPER HOLY AND INTELLIGENT FATHER GOD POSITIVE MADNESS OF THE HOLY SPIRIT OF TRUTH, ENYEN ODUDU ODUDU ODUDU ABASI MI OOO ZIM ZIM ZIM ASSASU, POSITIVE POSITIVE POSITIVE. UKEMEKE AKA IDIOK UNAM.

Let the peace and blessing of THE HOLY FATHER abide with everyone who corporates with this divine **FATHER'S TALK** (**GOD PRESENT**)

THANK YOU FATHER
BY
THE HOLY SPIRIT OF
THE FATHER GOD
THROUGH HIS SERVANT
The Senior Christ Servant
HRM King Solomon David Jesse **ETE**
Brotherhood of the
Cross and STAR
Eteroyal Universal family
Ikot Okwo The Great City of Refuge,
Ete Community
Ikot Abasi LGA-543001
Akwa Ibom State Nigeria-W/A
Tel. 08036693841
Website: www.ksslibrary.com
Email: ksslibrary@eteroyalmail.com

===============

READ AT LEAST SEVEN LECTURE REVELATIONS BEFORE YOU CAN MAKE ANY COMMENTS

In the Name of Our Lord Jesus Christ, In the Blood of Our Lord Jesus Christ, Now and forever more

Everybody should have access to and read at least seven **FATHER'S TALK**
(**GOD PRESENT**) Lecture Revelations before making any comments about it. If you do not go through at least seven **FATHER'S TALK** Lecture Revelations and you comment, you may make mistakes. And when you make mistakes your blood will be upon you because you would have taken voluntary evolution to misquote **THE**

FATHER GOD THE CREATOR OF THE UNIVERSE.

One of **THE FATHER'S TALK** stands for one SPIRIT of GOD, which means that THE **FATHER'S TALK (GOD PRESENT)** Lecture Revelations are witnessed by the Seven SPIRITS of GOD, which **I** use as the Seven Churches of GOD and Seven days of the Week, Seven spirits of Creation in one Supreme energy of **THE FATHER GOD**,

THE SPOKEN WORD therefore,

when you read seven **FATHER'S TALK (GOD PRESENT)** Lecture Revelations then, **I, THE FATHER GOD** will reveal you as a positive person and then you will have a portion in **ME**. And one of **THE FATHER'S TALK (GOD PRESENT)** will have a portion in you. Then you would know that this information came from **THE FATHER GOD. THE FATHER'S TALK (GOD PRESENT)** is not a mere talk from a man!

In the Name of Our Lord Jesus Christ, In the Blood of Our Lord Jesus Christ, Now and forever more

INVITATION

====

THE UNIVERSAL SUPREME ACKNOWLEDGEMENT

'THE ONLY SOURCE AND REMEDY TO END ALL HUMANITY PROBLEMS'

Join me to Celebrate; Acknowledge, Appreciate and give full RECOGNITION to THE UNIVERSAL SUPREME WORD,

> YOUR LIFE FORCE,
> THE TOTALITY OF ALL TOTALITIES
> YOUR CREATOR,
> THE FATHER GOD ALMIGHTY,
> THE CREATOR OF THE UNIVERSE

WWW.KSSLIBRARY.COM
WWW.COME4WORD.COM
WWW.THEWORDCITY.COM
WWW.KINGSOLOMONSPIRITUALLIBRARY.COM

Contact EMAIL:
hrmkingsolomon@eteroyalmail.com

THANK YOU FATHER

The title List of some of the
FATHER'S TALK
(GOD PRESENT)

1: THE MANUAL OF THE SPOKEN WORD

2: THE MANUAL OF LIFE

3: INVESTMENT WITH GOD

4: ISO IBOT EDEM IBOT

5: THE CHARACTER OF THE NEW WORLD

6: HELPMANTRANS

7: UNDERSTANDING MY WORD

8: TRUTH, POSITION, POST AND NAME

9: NON STOP BLESSING

10: IMPRESSION

11: STAGES OF EDUCATIONS (SPE, SSE & SUE)

12: THE ENGINEERING OF LIFE

13: THE CONTENT PACKAGE

14: THE BUDGET OF THE NEW WORLD

15: DIVINE ATTENTION

16: THE BABY SPIRIT

17: PROMOTION

18: ADVANCE AND PROGRESSING MIND

19: THE TEMPLE OF THE LIVING GOD

20: I AM OK

21: THE SPIRIT OF TRUTH

22: THE PERFECT PERMANENCY

23: THE FATHER GOD, GOD, GOD THE FATHER

24: HUSBAND, WIFE AND CHILD

25: GOD AND HIS HARBINGER

26: LIFE EVERLASTING

27: POSSESS

28: MY MIND AND MY PLAN

29: AFTER HEART AND AFTER MIND

30: MY DECLARATION & STAND IN BCS

31: BEYOND THE HOPE OF FAITH

32: MENTAL STAIN

33: THE PRINCIPLE OF SELF HOLD

34: THE MASTERSHIP

35: HIDU-CUM

36: THE UNIVERSAL PARENT

37: ADVANCED YOU AND ME

38: THE GREAT UNIVERSAL CHANGE

39: THE PROJECTED MIND
40: INDESTRUCTIBLE BLESSED FIVE STARS

41: ASTROTS, GOD PRESENT I AND MY FATHER

42: SONGS THE COMPLETION

43: THE RIGHT BUTTON

44: AKWA ABASI IBOM- ETE - DIRECTING NDITO AKWA IBOM

45: THE DIGITAL AGE

46: GOD IS OFFICIAL CHAMPION

47: A TRUE WITNESS

48: MYSTERY OF PROCREATION AND BIRTH

49: THE UNIVERSAL UMBRELLA

50: THE FORERUNNER

51: A OF A TO Z (FIRST OF ALL)

52: MAN IN THREE CAPACITIES

53: THE TRUE LIFE OF HOLY SPIRIT PERSONIFIED

54: IN-BETWEEN THE FATHER & THE SON

55: DIVINE ARRANGEMENT & AUTHORITY

56: TWENTY FIRST CENTURY IS NOT FOR SATAN

57: THE SUPREME WORD SEASON CELEBRATION

58: THE MAXIMUM DEITY

59: TRANSFORMER TRANSMITTER AND WAVE

60: THE SUPREME FUTURE

61: THE BYLOVE OF WORD

62: THE SIGNATURE OF THE FATHER GOD

63: THE TWO WAYS

64: THE UNDERSTANDING OF LIFE

65: THE GREATER THAN SOLOMON IS HERE

66: THE CONQUEROR

67: THE SPIRITUAL GENERAL INSPECTOR OF LIFE

68: THE NIGERIA IN THE AFRICA Part one

69: THE NIGERIA IN THE AFRICA Part two

70: THE CREATOR AND CREATIONS PART ONE

71: THE CREATOR AND CREATIONS PART TWO

72: THE CREATOR AND CREATIONS PART THREE

73: THE SUPREME TEACHER

74: THE SPIRITUAL COVER

75: THE NIGERIA IN THE AFRICA PART THREE

76: THE SUPREME BELIEVE

77: CAST AND BAN (LECTURE IN LIVERPOOL)

78: LIFE EXTENSION MANUAL

79: THE SPIRITUAL TRAFFIC

80: <u>THE VOICE OF THE CREATOR</u>

81: MY OFFICE

82: LIFE SPIRITUAL FIRE EXTINGUISHER

83: INFORMATION

84: FATHER GOD FINAL ARRANGEMENT

85: THE LOVERS OF CHRIST

86: I LOVE YOU, I LOVE YOU TOO

87: THE UNIVERSAL SUPREME UPDATE

88: THE SUPREME ALTAR

89: THE SOURCE AND DESTINATION

90: A SON LIKE THE FATHER THE KING OF KINGS A ROOTS FROM HEAVEN (NOT THIS TIME AROUND)

91: THE TRUE WITNESS AND THE TRUE SERVANT

92: THE FINAL ARRANGEMENT

93: A TRUE NIGERIAN MAN AND WOMAN

94: EVERYONE MUST PERSONALLY INVOLVE

95: BEWARE

96: ESIEN EMANA AKPAN "THE AFRICAN PROBLEMS"

97: THE SECRET OF THE UNIVERSAL PROBLEMS AND THE REMEDY (MUSLIM AND CHRISTIAN FROM THE SAME PARENT)

98: MMU-UDIM – THE BLESSED MOTHER (ABASI ME UDIM)

99: THINK WELL, SPEAK WELL AND DO WELL

100: THE STAGES OF HOW TO PROCESS THE WORD

101: EVIL STAIN, WHO RUNS AWAY FROM WHO

102: BEYOND HUMAN KNOW PURELY SPIRITUAL

103: <u>THE INSPIRATIONAL WRITER</u>

104: BIAKPAN OBIO AKPAN ABASI (THE NEW JERUSALEM CITY)

105: <u>"OBAMA" THE STRAINTHEN AND THE SPIRIT OF BILL GATES AND MICROSOFT</u>

THANK YOU FATHER

www.ingramcontent.com/pod-product-compliance
Lightning Source LLC
Chambersburg PA
CBHW021140230426
43667CB00005B/197